COUNSELING SKILLS
FOR
Companioning the Mourner

ALSO BY ALAN D. WOLFELT, PH.D., C.T.

Companioning the Bereaved: A Soulful Guide for Caregivers

Companioning the Grieving Child: A Soulful Guide for Caregivers

Loving from the Outside In, Mourning from the Inside Out

The Handbook for Companioning the Mourner:
Eleven Essential Principles

The Paradoxes of Mourning:
Healing Your Grief with Three Forgotten Truths

Understanding Your Grief:
Ten Essential Touchstones for Finding Hope and Healing Your Heart

Companion
P R E S S

Companion Press is dedicated to the education and support of both the
bereaved and bereavement caregivers. We believe that those who companion
the bereaved by walking with them as they journey in grief have a wondrous
opportunity: to help others embrace and grow through grief—and to lead fuller,
more deeply-lived lives themselves because of this important ministry.

For a complete catalog and ordering information, write, call, or visit:

Companion Press
The Center for Loss and Life Transition
3735 Broken Bow Road | Fort Collins, CO 80526
(970) 226-6050 | www.centerforloss.com

COUNSELING SKILLS
FOR
Companioning the Mourner

THE FUNDAMENTALS OF EFFECTIVE GRIEF COUNSELING

ALAN D. WOLFELT, PH.D., C.T.

Companion
PRESS

An imprint of the Center for Loss and Life Transition
Fort Collins, Colorado

Companion Press is an imprint of the Center for Loss and Life Transition,
3735 Broken Bow Road, Fort Collins, Colorado 80526.

26   25   24   23   22   5   4   3   2   1

ISBN: 978-1-61722-324-2

To the children, teens, adults, and families who have allowed me the honor of providing them a safe place to mourn well, so they can live well and love well.

CONTENTS

INTRODUCTION

I REMIND MYSELF FREQUENTLY THAT BEREAVEMENT LITERALLY MEANS "TO BE TORN APART" AND "TO HAVE SPECIAL NEEDS." When a fellow human being's life has been torn apart by the death of someone loved, she deserves to be surrounded by caring, compassionate people who are good grief companions.

"To comfort me, you have to come close. Come sit with me on my mourning bench."

— NICHOLAS WOLTERSTOFF, *LAMENT FOR A SON*

The impetus for this book came from the observation that many people surrounding mourners are knowledgeable about grief and the need to mourn but often lack the helping skills to, well, help. To artfully companion people experiencing profound loss requires high levels of interpersonal counseling skills.

My hope is that the contents of this resource will be of value to both the student just starting out in grief care as well as the experienced counselor. Because it covers both philosophical underpinnings and the how-tos of fundamental skills, it will be useful to people continuing on for professional training in grief counseling and to people in paraprofessional or peer support settings, as well as to those who find themselves in informal helping relationships in their day-to-day lives.

For the grief support beginner, this resource is intended to provide a solid foundation in essential helping skills. For the experienced grief counselor, this resource will assist in articulating philosophies of grief care, reviewing and possibly honing current skills, adding new skills, and enhancing continued growth as a caregiver.

As someone who has a passion for training grief support persons and counselors, I work from the conviction that all interpersonal relationships are either helpful (growth-enhancing), neutral (neither helpful nor harmful), or harmful (destructive). I also believe that skills in responding supportively to people experiencing grief and the need to mourn are not innate but learned through modeling and focused practice. This book provides principles, practical skills, and activities whose aim is to enhance your capacity to facilitate ("to make easer") the hard work of mourning. I also include an introductory overview of my philosophical approach of "companioning" versus "treating" mourners. In essence, the contents of this primer are directed at people in grief care, with the goal of adding to their toolbox of helping skills and inspiring them to be truly helpful caregivers.

I do ask you to keep in mind that grief counseling is a vast subject. There is no shortcut to becoming an effective grief-care provider. While this training resource will help you learn counseling skills related to your interest in providing grief support, my intent is not, nor should it be, to make you a grief therapist. I encourage those of you interested in becoming professional counselors to find a training program that meets your needs and career aspirations and meets the requirements of the state in which you live.

While you may read this book and work on the skills it reviews on your own, your concurrent participation in a workshop or classroom setting with an experienced trainer is strongly recommended. For example, I myself have taught for many years a four-day training entitled Counseling Skills Fundamentals, for which this book will soon serve as the companion text. The opportunity to participate with others and to share experiences has proved to be invaluable for caregivers who want to enhance their grief counseling skills. Increased understanding typically comes from discussions, modeling, and group experiences, rather than simply reading the text. We would love for you to come join us for our annual training on this topic!

Enjoy, and I hope we meet one day.

Alan D. Wolfelt, Ph.D., C.T.
September 2015

PART ONE:

THE STARTING POINT

WHERE DOES EFFECTIVE GRIEF CARE START? IT STARTS WITH YOU, THE CAREGIVER.

It starts with what you believe about grief and mourning.

It starts with your training and understanding of the helping relationship.

> *"What I can do is offer myself, wholehearted and present, to walk through the fear and the mess. That's all any of us can do. That's what we're here for."*
>
> — SHAUNA NIEQUIST

It starts with your innate personality.

It starts with your personal experiences with loss and grief.

It starts with how all of this translates into your ways of being when you are in the company of someone who is grieving.

Whenever you enter into a counseling relationship, you are about to embark on a journey through the wilderness of grief with a fellow human being. You might think of the starting point as the trailhead. Before you set off, I urge you to make sure you are as prepared as possible. The wilderness is vast and inhospitable, and the journey is grueling. The mourner is trusting in you to help him survive.

Yes, lives are at stake—usually not literal life-or-death

consequences but instead what I consider the even more important life of the soul.

On the journey to come, you will not be the guide, exactly, because (if you agree with me about my companioning philosophy of grief care, which we'll soon talk more about) you will be walking alongside the mourner, not in front of or behind him. As you walk, you will be allowing the mourner to choose the path. After all, this is really his journey—not yours.

But as his trusted and discerning companion, you are tasked with helping him discover paths that lead to healing. You will help him read the compass and look for the signposts that are the six needs of mourning. You will try to ensure adequate shelter (safe places to express thoughts and feelings), food (regular meals of compassion and hope), and water (recognizing what sustains him day to day). You will watch out for the hazards of complicated grief and learn when to refer him to another helper when his needs are beyond your training and experience. While you are not responsible *for* him, you are responsible *to* him for all of these things.

"Grief is not a disorder, a disease, or a sign of weakness. It is an emotional, physical, and spiritual necessity, the price you pay for love. The only cure for grief is to grieve."

— RABBI EARL GROLLMAN

Helping people who are grieving—and helping people who help people who are grieving—is my life's work. This book starts at the trailhead of grief and is meant to help you be as prepared for and capable of truly helping mourners as possible.

GRIEF AND MOURNING: FOUNDATIONAL BELIEFS

Like my colleague and friend Rabbi Grollman, I believe that grief is normal and necessary. It is not, as the medical model of grief care implies, an illness that must be cured or a pathology that must be treated. Instead, it is the natural process of integrating losses of all kinds that we as conscious, complex human beings can't help but experience in life.

We grieve whenever something or someone we value and are attached to is taken away from us. And so we grieve during and after divorce. We grieve after significant life transitions, such as going off to college or to live on our own, milestone birthdays, and leaving a job we care about. Perhaps most significantly, we grieve after someone we love dies.

All of these common life experiences (and many others) are, at least in part, losses. And losses naturally engender grief.

Essentially, grief is what we think and feel inside after a loss. Grief isn't just sadness, of course. Often, it is also feelings of shock, denial, disorganization, confusion, anger, fear, and panic. It can include regret and sometimes relief. It may be physical pain and social discomfort. It can be disjointed thinking and spiritual despair. It is physical, cognitive, emotional, social, and spiritual.

Grief is all of that and more.

Mourning, on the other hand, is the expression of those thoughts and feelings outside of ourselves. Mourning is how we heal our grief.

And in the helping relationship, mourning is where *you* come in.

Your role in helping people who are grieving is to provide a safe place and empathetic presence in which they can honestly, openly, and fully mourn. A sanctuary, if you will. You normalize and affirm.

You bear witness and encourage. And most of all, you listen.

I have written extensively about the fundamentals of grief and mourning in many other resources, so I will not go into more depth or detail about them here. For the purposes of this book—and to help you ready yourself for the trailhead—it is simply enough for you to understand what I mean by grief and mourning...and by grief companioning.

MY COMPANIONING PHILOSOPHY OF GRIEF CARE

I am a passionate believer in and supporter of grief counseling, both professional counseling and lay support. That's because mourning—which, remember, is the expression of grief outside oneself and is the very key to healing—is mostly not a solo experience.

While some methods of expressing grief can be accomplished alone—such as crying, journaling, and participating in spiritual activities like meditation or prayer—mourning often requires the compassionate, nonjudgmental presence of at least one other human being. And in our mourning-avoidant culture, such a person is rare indeed.

The most fundamental and essential way to mourn is to talk to a good listener about your inner thoughts and feelings. (Whether they realize it or not, all good grief listeners are basically grief counselors.) And so we need effective grief counselors. Lots and lots of them. Trouble is, the medical model of grief care that educates and prepares professional grief counselors (including psychiatrists, psychologists, social workers, and other mental health caregivers) too often does an unsatisfactory job, in my opinion, of preparing them well for the trailhead.

Very early on—in my childhood, actually—I understood that I wanted to be a grief counselor. So after finishing my undergraduate degree, I earned a master's in psychology and then a doctorate. I completed my internship in clinical psychology at the Mayo Clinic. During these years, I also began to counsel grieving families, so that I could learn up close from grievers and those who care for them.

Grieving people taught me a lot about authentic grief and mourning—both then and in the nearly 40 years since I've spent as a grief counselor and educator. What my formal schooling tried to teach me, on the other hand, was often less helpful. You see, according to the medical model of psychological theory, grief can be considered an illness that with proper assessment, diagnosis, and treatment can be cured.

I've always found it intriguing that the word "treat" comes from the Latin root word *tractare*, which means "to drag." If we combine that with "patient," we can really get in trouble. "Patient" means "passive long-term sufferer," so if we treat patients, we drag passive, long-term sufferers. Simply stated, that's not very empowering.

> *"When we honestly ask ourselves which person in our lives means the most to us, we often find that it is those who, instead of giving advice, solutions, or cures, have chosen rather to share our pain and touch our wounds with a gentle and tender hand. The friend who can be silent with us in a moment of despair or confusion, who can stay with us in an hour of grief or bereavement, who can tolerate not knowing, not curing, not healing, and face with us the reality of our powerlessness, that is a friend who cares."*
>
> — HENRI NOUWEN

In my grief counseling philosophy, in lieu of the word "treat," I use "companion." When broken down into its original Latin roots, it means "messmate": *com* for "with" and *pan* for "bread." Someone you would share a meal with, a friend, an equal. I have taken liberties with the noun "companion" and made it into the verb "companioning" because it so well captures the type of grief counseling relationship I support and advocate. In fact, that is the very image of companioning—sitting together, being present to one another, sharing, communing, abiding in the fellowship of hospitality.

"Wisdom is not a product of schooling but of the lifelong attempt to acquire it."

— ALBERT EINSTEIN

Companioning people in grief is therefore not about assessing, analyzing, fixing, or resolving another's grief. Instead, it is about being totally present to the mourner—even being a temporary guardian of her soul.

The companioning model is anchored in a "teach-me" perspective. It is about learning and observing. In fact, the meaning of "observance" comes to us from ritual. It means not only to "watch out for" but also "to keep and honor," "to bear witness." The caregiver's awareness of this need to learn is the essence of true companioning.

MY 11 TENETS OF "COMPANIONING" VERSUS TREATING PEOPLE IN GRIEF

1. Companioning is about being present to another person's pain; it is not about taking away the pain.

2. Companioning is about going to the wilderness of the soul with another human being; it is not about thinking you are responsible for finding the way out.

3. Companioning is about honoring the spirit; it is not about focusing on the intellect.

4. Companioning is about listening with the heart; it is not about analyzing with the head.

5. Companioning is about bearing witness to the struggles of others; it is not about judging or directing these struggles.

6. Companioning is about walking alongside; it is not about leading.

7. Companioning is about discovering the gifts of sacred silence; it is not about filling up every moment with words.

8. Companioning is about being still; it is not about frantic movement forward.

9. Companioning is about respecting disorder and confusion; it is not about imposing order and logic.

10. Companioning is about learning from others; it is not about teaching them.

11. Companioning is about compassionate curiosity; it is not about expertise.

If your desire is to support a fellow human in grief, you must create a "safe place" for people to embrace their feelings of profound loss. More than a comfortable office, this safe place is a cleaned-out, compassionate heart. It is the open heart that allows you to be truly present to another human being's intimate pain.

As a caregiver to mourners, I am a companion, not a "guide"— which assumes a knowledge of another's soul I cannot claim. Neither am I an expert. To companion our fellow humans means to watch and learn.

"Eating, and any hospitality in general, is a communion."
— JESSE BROWNER

A central role of the companion to mourners involves the art of honoring stories. Honoring stories requires that we slow down, turn inward, and really listen as people acknowledge the reality of loss, embrace pain, review memories, and search for meaning.

The philosophy and practice of companioning also interfaces naturally with the art of hospitality. Hospitality is the essence of knowing how to live in society. Among the ancient Greeks, hospitality was a necessary element of day-to-day life. In a land where borders were permeable, it was important to get to know one's neighbors as potential friends.

One way to do this was to share meals together. First, the guest and host would pour a libation to the gods. Then they would eat ("break bread") together. Then, after the guest had his fill, they would tell each other their stories, with the guest going first. Often, tears were shed because their stories were highly personal: battles, family histories, and life tragedies were recounted. After the evening together, the host and guest were potential allies. Still today, breaking bread and sharing personal stories are key elements of companioning people through death and grief.

The spiritual thinker Henri Nouwen once elegantly described hospitality as the "creation of a free space where the stranger can enter and become a friend instead of an enemy." He observed that hospitality is not about trying to change people, but instead about offering them space where change can take place. He astutely noted, "Hospitality is not a subtle invitation to adopt the lifestyle of the host, but the gift of a chance for the guest to find his own."

And while we're talking about terms, let's consider the word "client," too. Coming from the Latin for "obey" or "incline or bend," it is another power word. I do not treat patients or clients. Rather, I companion my fellow human beings who are experiencing natural, necessary grief.

To reinforce the importance of the companioning philosophy of grief care, throughout the rest of this book, I will use the term "companion" interchangeably with the word "counselor" and I will avoid the use of the terms "patient" and "client."

OTHER MODELS OF CAREGIVING AND THEORIES OF BEREAVEMENT

I believe it is critically important to familiarize yourself with different grief models and theories. The body of knowledge in thanatology is actually very new, and we have more to learn. Beyond the general helping skills literature, there is a unique body of mysterious knowledge that has important application to grief caregiving. While I have attempted to provide leadership and advocacy for a model of "companioning" my fellow human beings in grief, we must also acknowledge that no one model can take into account all the aspects of helping the mourner.

I would encourage you to read and reflect on various models and see what resonates with you in your caregiving efforts. See the Recommended

Reading list on page 123. Learn about attachment theory (Bowlby, 1982), the continuing bonds theory (Klass, Silverman, Nickman, 1996), the task-based model of grief (Rando, 1993; Worden, 2008), the two-track model of bereavement (Rubin, 1999), the dual-process model (Stroebe, Schut, Stroebe, 2005), the meaning reconstruction and growth model (Atig, 1996), the disenfranchisement model (Doka, 2002), as well as the companioning model (Wolfelt, 2005).

Being an open learner and knowing you will never arrive at being a "grief expert" will encourage you to keep learning from various researchers, academicians, and clinicians in the area of death education and counseling.

MORE COMPANIONING PREPARATION FOR THE TRAILHEAD

I believe that every grief caregiver must work to develop his or her own theory or point of view about what helps people who are grieving. Challenging yourself to explain what happens in your caregiving relationships with grieving people and families will, in my experience, assist you in understanding and improving the results of the important work you do.

Developing your own grief care precepts facilitates a coherence of ideas about the helping process and also generates new ideas about how to be helpful. Outlined below are 20 principles that undergird *my* work. My hope is that you will also challenge yourself to write out *your* philosophy of effective caregiving to people in grief.

1. Bereavement, grief, and mourning are normal and necessary experiences; however, they are often traumatic and transformative. I convey a deep respect for grief and mourning to the mourner, thus enabling her to convert her grief into authentic mourning.

2. The helping process is seen as a collaborative, "companioning"

process among people. The traditional medical model of mental health care is inadequate and complicating. As a companion, I try to create conditions that engage people actively in the reconciliation needs of mourning. I provide a "helping alliance" with the mourner that is focused on her needs.

3. True expertise in grief or death lies with (and only with) the unique person who is grieving. Only he can be the expert. The companion is there to learn from the griever and to bear witness to and normalize his journey.

4. The foundation upon which helping grieving people takes place is in the context of an encouraging, hope-filled relationship between the companion and the mourner. The widely acknowledged core conditions of helping (empathy, warmth and caring, genuineness, respect) are seen as essential ingredients in working with grieving people and families.

5. Traditional mental health diagnostic categories are seen as limitations on the helping process. The concept of "gardening" as opposed to "assessing" better describes efforts to understand the meaning of the journey in the grieving person's life. I strive to understand not only the potential complications of the journey, but also individual strengths and levels of wellness.

6. The counseling model is holistic in nature and views grieving people as physical, cognitive, emotional, social, and spiritual beings. Each person is unique and seeks not just to "be" but to become.

7. The underlying theoretical model is systems-oriented and sees the grieving person as being a node in a web of interdependent relationships with society and other people, groups, and institutions.

8. The focus of companioning grieving people is balanced between

the past, the present, and the future. Learning about past life experiences (particularly family of origin influences) and the nature of important relationships among the mourner and the important people in her life helps me understand the meaning of the grief and mourning process for this unique person.

9. A grieving person's perception of her reality *is* her reality. A "here and now" understanding of that reality allows me to be with her where she is instead of trying to push her somewhere she is not. I will be a more effective helper if I remember to enter into a person's feelings without having a need to change her feelings.

10. A major helping goal is to provide a "safe place" for grieving people to do the work of mourning, resulting in healing and growth. The grieving person does not have an illness I need to cure. I'm a caregiver, not a cure-giver!

11. People are viewed from a multicultural perspective. What is considered "normal" in one culture may be perceived as "abnormal" in another culture. On a shrinking planet, my caring and concern must be global in its perspective.

12. Spiritual and religious concerns and needs are seen as central to the reconciliation process. To be an effective companion, I must be tuned in to helping people grow in depth and vitality in their spiritual and religious lives as they search for meaning and purpose in their continued living.

13. Men and women are seen in androgynous ways that encourage understanding beyond traditional sex-role stereotypes. Artful companions understand that bonded relationships exist outside the boundaries of traditional male-female partnerships and marriage.

14. The overall goal of helping grieving people is reconciliation, not resolution. As a companion, I have a responsibility not to help them return to an "old normal," but instead to discover how loss changes them in many different ways. Traditional mental health models that teach resolution as the helping goal are seen as self-limiting and potentially destructive to grievers.

15. Right-brain methods of healing and growth (intuitive, metaphoric) are seen as valuable and are integrated with left-brain methods (intentional, problem-solving approaches). This synergy encourages a more growth-filled approach to grief caregiving than do historical mental health models (primarily based on left-brain methods) of caregiving.

16. "Complicated" mourning is perceived as blocked growth. The "complicated mourner" probably simply needs help in understanding the central needs of mourning and how to embrace them in ways that help him heal. Most people are where they are in their grief journeys for one of two major reasons: 1) That is where they need to be at this point in their journey; or 2) They need, yet lack, an understanding, safe place for mourning and a person who can help facilitate their work of mourning in more growth-producing, hope-filled ways.

17. Helping avenues must be adapted to the unique needs of the grieving person. Some people are responsive to group work, some to individual work, and some to family systems work. Many people are best served, in fact, by seeking support from lay companions who have walked before them in the grief journey.

18. There is a commitment to using educational, primary prevention efforts to impact societal change because we live in

a "mourning-avoiding" culture. I have a responsibility to inform other people throughout the world of the need to create safe places for people to mourn in healthy ways.

19. There is a responsibility to create conditions for healing to take place in the grieving person. The ultimate responsibility for eventual healing lies within the person. I must remember to be responsible *to* grieving people, not responsible *for* them.

20. Excellent self-care is essential, for it provides the physical, cognitive, emotional, social, and spiritual renewal necessary for me to be an effective, ongoing companion in grief.

If you'd like to learn more about the companioning philosophy of grief care, I encourage you to read my book *Companioning the Bereaved: A Soulful Guide for Caregivers*. While it does not cover the foundational helping skills that are the subject of Part Two of this resource, it does further examine, one by one, the companioning tenets listed on page 11, providing you with a more in-depth theoretical framework.

GRIEF CARE: A UNIQUE FORM OF CAREGIVING

It has always captured my attention that many people become counselors because of a significant life transition of their own, whether the death of a loved one, a divorce, job loss, empty-nest challenges, or another major loss. Yet many counselor education programs offer little in the way of grief care training—perhaps a short unit that might as well be entitled "We covered grief today."

So we must learn more about grief on our own. Compassionate grief companions spend time learning the mysterious body of knowledge about grief and mourning and then add high-level helping skills to the mix.

To provide heart-centered caregiving demands an understanding of grief as a normal, adaptive response and not as a pathology that requires "treatment." Grief is not something we as humans "resolve," "let go of," or "overcome." Those of us who companion the grieving come to realize that while the unfolding process involves pain and genuine suffering, the helping goal is to facilitate—literally, "to make easier." We affirm for mourners that while we see that they are in the dark and will be with them there, we also know that they can and will emerge into the light. What a true honor to companion one's fellow human beings!

> *"Always remember that for each person you see, you may be the only person in their life capable of both hearing and holding their pain. If that isn't sacred, I don't know what is."*
>
> — AUTHOR UNKNOWN

WHAT *YOU* BRING TO THE TRAILHEAD

Now that we've reviewed the basics of grief and mourning and explored the companioning philosophy of grief caregiving, it's time to look at the other essential and inextricable piece you bring with you to the trailhead: yourself.

> *"Knowing yourself is the beginning of all wisdom."*
>
> — ARISTOTLE

You come to your role as grief companion not as a blank slate but as a human being who has already experienced and learned much, who has lived and loved...and lost.

You were raised by a family from whom you gleaned a defining understanding of how the world works. And you were also born a human being at a certain moment in time with a unique genetic make-up and a one-of-a-kind soul.

Because every person is unique, every grief companion is unique. There is no one right way of acting, thinking, speaking, or being in the helping relationship. Still, we all know people who are naturally good helpers and who, with continued training and experience, grow to become exceptional grief companions.

I have found that remarkable grief companions share five essential attributes:

FIVE ESSENTIAL ATTRIBUTES FOR GRIEF COMPANIONS

1. *A belief in self as instrument*
   Are you congruently matched to this work?
   - Personality
   - Life experiences
   - Strengths and weaknesses

2. *Empathetic relationship qualities*
   Are you naturally good at the core conditions/qualities of helping?
   - Sensitivity and warmth
   - Communication of acceptance
   - Desire to understand

3. *An open learner orientation*
   Are you interested in the mysterious body of knowledge surrounding grief and loss (such as misconceptions about grief, unique influences on mourning, dimensions of the grief response, the six central needs of mourning, complicated mourning and its subcategories, criteria for reconciliation, self-care knowledge and skills, and when to refer)? Are you also open to being taught by each unique mourner?

4. *Effective basic counseling skills*

Are you interested in learning and practicing high-level helping skills to facilitate the six reconciliation needs of mourning?

- Attending
- Paraphrasing
- Clarifying
- Perception checking
- Leading
- Questioning
- Reflecting feelings
- Confronting
- Summarizing

5. *A commitment to good self-care*

Are you committed to caring for yourself even as you care for others?

Let's briefly discuss each of these attributes in an effort to help you discern whether or not you are well suited to grief caregiving as well as which areas you may want to focus your self-improvement efforts on.

1. A belief in self as instrument

In the mid-1900s, humanist thinker and educational theorist Arthur Wright Combs proposed a helping concept he called "self as instrument." By this he meant that teachers and other helpers and caregivers are not simply indistinguishable technicians who deliver services mechanically or uniformly. Rather, they are unique individuals who use their whole selves to shape and funnel the care or services they provide. Not only are their methods unique, their interactions are also highly tailored to the needs and personalities of each unique person in their care.

Caregivers who see themselves as instruments in their work are creative, adaptable, and passionate. Grief companions with the self-as-instrument mindset are congruently suited to the role. Their inner beliefs and passions align strongly with the companioning philosophy. Their personalities as well as innate strengths and weaknesses make them good listeners and helpers. They also often have life experiences that have sensitized them to loss and grief and the importance of compassionate grief support.

2. **Empathetic relationship qualities**

Effective grief companions are sensitive and warm. While they may exhibit these qualities in various ways, the net result is the same: other people perceive them as compassionate, welcoming, and easy to be around.

Another important facet of empathy for effective grief companions is acceptance. They take people as they come. They do not judge or dictate. Instead, they seek to understand each unique individual, and they communicate that acceptance through all of the helping skills we will review in Part Two.

3. **An open learner orientation**

Humbleness and unquenchable curiosity are the hallmarks of the open learner—and the good grief companion. Open learners know that they will always have more to learn about grief and mourning, and they proactively seek out this understanding in a variety of ways, including reading seminal and new texts, attending lectures and workshops, participating in peer groups, and taking advantage of educational opportunities whenever they arise.

A "teach-me" attitude is also essential for grief companions.

Instead of setting out to teach the mourners in their care, they plan on learning from their unique stories and experiences.

4. **Effective basic counseling skills**

   Effective grief companions are more than willing to lean the effective counseling skills we will review in Part Two of this resource, and because they are passionate about being the best helpers they can be, they also never cease to work at improving their fundamental counseling skills.

5. **A commitment to good self-care**

   You've heard the saying, "You can't help others unless you first help yourself." It's true, of course. Not only do you need and deserve excellent self-care, but you also owe it to the fellow human beings you are companioning through grief. If you are fatigued, depleted, and frazzled, you simply cannot be effectively and compassionately present to mourners.

The main purpose of this book is to cover the "how tos" of numbers 2 and 4, above—empathetic relationship qualities and effective basic counseling skills. As a lead-in to those topics, we've also reviewed the fundamentals of the companioning philosophy, which overlaps quite a bit with number 1, a belief in self as instrument. And we'll be talking a bit more about number 5, self-care, in Part Three of this resource.

But there's one more important trailhead subtopic that we need to touch on before we dive into empathy and counseling skills: life experiences and personal loss history. Effective grief companions not only believe in and nurture self as instrument, they also seek to understand how their personal loss histories and motivations as caregivers factor into their work with their grieving fellow human beings.

DO I REALLY WANT TO BE A GRIEF COMPANION?

1. Can I be a "safe harbor"—a dependable, non-judgmental companion to this person?

2. Can I be with people who are hurting and in pain?

3. Can I attempt to see the world through the eyes of this person?

4. Do people perceive my desire to understand them? More importantly, do I have the desire to understand them and a willingness to be taught?

5. Am I able to pull back and know I need "time outs" from companioning others from time to time? Am I able to sense when my bucket is low and needs to be filled?

6. Do I understand my separateness as a person? Am I able to maintain boundaries in this relationship?

7. Can I respect my own needs while focusing on the needs of others?

8. Am I able to free myself from the need to diagnose, evaluate, and assess? Can I instead see myself more as an explorer who sets out with the mourner to see what we discover?

9. Can I see this person as someone who is becoming rather than as a static person, bound by their past or present?

10. Am I able to confront people in a supportive way when the need arises?

Asking these questions of yourself and honestly answering them will help you discern whether or not you are well suited to grief companioning. While it is true that you can learn and develop your helping skills, it is also true that not everyone is naturally a good grief companion. Don't feel ashamed if you decide that you're not a good fit for this work. If you still want to be of service, there are many other rewarding and essential ways you can support your fellow human beings. I encourage you to follow your impulse for compassion wherever it leads.

NINE MORE QUALITIES OF EFFECTIVE HELPERS

In addition to the five essential attributes for grief companions we reviewed on page 20, here are some more qualities that effective grief companions usually have in spades.

1. *Respectfulness*

   This important quality relates to a non-possessive caring for and affirmation of the mourner as a separate, equal person capable of healing from the inside out. Respect involves a receptive attitude of having the mourner teach you about her experience of grief. The opposite of this respectful, companioning stance would be the caregiver who presumptuously believes that her superior knowledge of grief qualifies her to project what is best for the mourner to think, feel, and do.

2. *Genuineness*

   The grief companion must truly be himself—non-phony and non-defensive. His words and actions match his inner feelings. Genuineness results in interpersonal richness. When the mourner senses you are genuine, she feels safe to be genuine, too.

3. *Trustworthiness*

   Trust is about consistency and safety. Grieving people often naturally feel a lack of trust in the world after the death of someone loved. They sometimes wonder if they should risk trusting or caring again. As a companion, you have an obligation to help the mourner feel consistently safe with you. When trust forms between two people, there is a palpable exchange of energy. And conversely, when trust is lacking or absent, no energy is exchanged and nothing happens.

4. *Immediacy*

   This quality has to do with being present to the mourner in the here and now. It goes beyond the content of what is being said to the process of what is happening from moment to moment. The high-functioning companion has the gift of high levels of immediacy. The mourner's needs are right there in the present moment, and immediacy allows you to be empathetically responsive to those needs. The present moment is where the needs of the soul reside—and grief work is anchored in soul work.

5. *Humility*

   The humble grief companion exudes a willingness to learn from her own mistakes as well as an appreciation of her limitations and strengths. Humility also means continually being aware of how your own experiences with loss are impacting your presence to the mourner.

"If we can give up attachment to our role as helpers, then maybe our clients can give up attachment to their roles as patients and we can meet as fellow souls on this incredible journey."

— RAM DASS

Helpers who are humble remember to ask questions of themselves, such as, "How am I being impacted by sharing in the mourner's experiences with grief?" "Does the mourner's experience with loss remind me of some of my own losses?" "Where can I share the feelings that supporting this mourner stimulates in me?" Humility also means that you are not the expert but are open to learning what each new companioning relationship has to teach you about being helpful at this moment in time. And humility interfaces with developing a service ethic—genuinely wanting to care for others while at the same time realizing you are not "in charge." Instead, you submit yourself to the tenets of companioning and open your soul to the mysterious journey called grief.

6. *Concreteness*

When you are concrete, you communicate clearly and specifically with mourners. You strive to be definite and understandable rather than vague and general. Counselor-speak labeling is a good example of the vagueness and ambiguity you want to avoid. While it may seem safe and convey expertise to use terms like "passive-aggressive" or "transference" when you are summarizing for the mourner, those are not concrete or understandable words. Instead, explain in specific, lay-friendly language. Also, using concreteness sometimes means gently prompting the mourner to be more specific when he is being vague or generalizing.

7. *Potency*

This quality has to do with the grief companion's confidence and charisma. Potent companions have presence and serve as models for effective living. Potent companions are comfortable with themselves and invite others to experience the same comfortableness. But wait—aren't confidence and charisma the opposite of humility? Yes and no. Being egotistical and arrogant are not acceptable qualities in grief companions, but conveying confidence in the helping relationship and enthusiasm for the work you do together are. Do you see the difference?

8. *Humor*

Even in the midst of grief, moments of levity and humor spontaneously occur. How much lighter we feel when we laugh in the midst of our pain. Too much unrelenting sitting in despair and seriousness violates the laws of the universe. It's important for mourners to dose themselves with pain, interspersing the hurt with stretches of other activities and feelings, including laughter and joy. The effective grief companion knows when and how to appropriately use humor in the relationship and is comfortable with laughter when it erupts.

9. *Heart*

To have "heart" as you companion people in grief is to be true to your own feelings, humanness, and vulnerabilities. When you work from a place of heart, you function as a whole. When your analytical, thinking self is in charge, you may be just in your head. Yet the centerpiece of the integration of grief is not the mind but the heart. Being a companion naturally occurs when you relax into yourself and bring compassion to all of your helping efforts. When you minister from the heart, you are in a state of deep connection with the divine, with yourself, and with other human beings.

We will talk about empathy, patience, and hopefulness later in this book, as well, for of course these are also essential qualities in the effective grief companion.

EXPLORING YOUR PERSONAL LOSS BACKGROUND, CURRENT ISSUES, AND MOTIVATIONS

To companion your fellow human beings during times of grief and loss, you must stay very self-aware of your own issues. Working in this area of caregiving puts you face-to-face with your own fears of losses of all kinds, especially the deaths of people close to you, not to mention your own mortality.

What's more, the grief and mourning of the fellow human beings in your care naturally conjure your thoughts, feelings, and memories related to past losses in your life. There is no such thing as being a grief companion without also simultaneously re-experiencing your own griefs, at least to some degree.

Allow me to provide a framework for you to explore three important areas of loss self-awareness:

1. *Your background related to death and life losses*
   As caregivers we come from all sorts of different backgrounds and life experiences. Each of us comes from our own unique family of origin and cultural context. Some of us have a history of loss (it is true that your greatest gifts often come from your wounds), while others do not. Some of the families we were raised in were open and honest about death and grief, while others tried to deny or go around grief instead of through it.

   To enhance your awareness of your experiences with grief and loss and the ways in which your attitudes have been shaped, please explore the following questions:

   > *"Compassion is not a relationship between the healer and the wounded. It's a relationship between equals. Only when we know our own darkness well can we be present with the darkness of others. Compassion becomes real when we recognize our shared humanity."*
   > — PEMA CHODRON

   - What was your first experience with death? What thoughts and feelings did you have at that time?
   - How did your family, friends, and other significant people in your life respond at that time?
   - What do you recall as you reflect backward on this experience?
   - How were death and grief handled in your family of origin?

- Were they discussed openly and honestly?

- Were they considered taboo topics?

- How did your family's treatment of death and grief impact you?

- Do you recall experiencing the death of companion animals in your family? What was that like for you? Was your family supportive of your need to mourn?

- What experiences with funerals have you had?

- If the first funeral you experienced was as a child, were you nurtured by adults around you? Did you feel a sense of inclusion or exclusion from funeral experiences as a child?

- What childhood experiences did you have of being in the presence of dead bodies? What was that like for you?

- How did your family's religious, cultural, and ethnic background influence your experiences with death?

- What is your understanding of how your early experiences with death influenced your life?

- What other losses have you had in your life (divorce, moves, job loss, etc.)? Were you able to mourn these life transitions?

- Of the people in your life who are still alive, which ones' deaths would be the most difficult for you? Why do you think that is?

- When do you think it is appropriate to share your own loss experiences with grieving people you companion?

2. *Your current personal issues surrounding grief and loss*
   As you companion your fellow human beings in loss, you naturally reflect on your own life losses. Your personal history of loss can help or, at times (if you yourself don't practice what you believe about the need to mourn), hinder your caregiving efforts.

As I've said, we can never take anyone any further than we go ourselves. Therefore, we must always stay conscious of our own mourning needs.

When we experience losses in our own lives, it's time to step back and tend to our own grief. Obviously, there is no shame in seeking support and doing our own mourning. If we don't, there is a risk that we will project our own issues into the helping relationship and unconsciously try to meet our own needs for support and understanding. Be sure you have a "responsibility partner" who can help you discern where you are with your grief journeys.

Conversely, some people project that when we as caregivers experience life losses, we lose objectivity and are unable to assist others. I totally disagree! As long as we do our own grief work, the losses that touch our lives can actually heighten our empathy and result in greater depth of understanding. But a warning: Always be sure to separate your needs from the needs of those you have the honor of companioning.

Of course, the nature of our work does expose us to more loss than most people. We are at risk for "bereavement overload," in which our lives are overfull with grief. Again, ongoing support and the use of a "responsibility partner" are vital to good self-companionship. Don't be surprised if, from time to time, you need a mini-sabbatical away from death, dying, grief, and loss. There is no shame in taking this time away, only wise discernment!

Make use of the following questions to assist you in looking at your current personal loss issues:

- Which personal losses are currently influencing your life

journey? What are you doing with these losses? Whom do you turn to for support surrounding these losses? Where do you see yourself in integrating these losses into your life?

- Who serves as your "responsibility partner"? How often do you see this person? How do you make use of your time together?

- Do you have any sense that you may project your own loss issues into the work you do to help others? If so, how so? If not, why not? What do you do to have clarity around "your" life issues versus "their" life issues?

- Have you ever experienced "loss overload"? If so, what have you done to acknowledge this and take care of yourself? How often are you able to go to exile and be away from loss and grief?

3. *Your motivations as a caregiver*

My experience suggests that people go into this rewarding but stressful area of caregiving for a multitude of different reasons. Regardless of your unique motivations, I believe it is important to explore and understand them.

Caring for mourners tends to draw people who care deeply about people, are highly motivated to help others, and are often idealistic, expecting this area of caregiving to give them a tremendous sense of meaning and purpose. This is particularly true of those who see this work as a "calling" (a concept I believe in and identify with myself, by the way, but a concept that can also put those of us who are called at risk of burnout).

Some caregivers enter into the profession wanting to "rescue" people from distress, pain, and suffering. Similarly, our understanding of what constitutes "healthy mourning"—and whether we've helped those in our care achieve it—can affect our feelings of success or failure as caregivers to grieving people. While I am certainly an advocate for helping those in grief meet the six needs of mourning (more on that in the next section), I am at risk for the same disillusion, disappointment, frustration, and sense of failure if I believe myself responsible for these outcomes.

Make use of the following questions to assist you in exploring your motivations as a grief caregiver:

- How would you describe your motivation to work in this area of caregiving? What is the most rewarding aspect of what you do? What is the most stressful aspect of what you do?

- Does this work provide you with a sense of meaning and purpose? If so, why do you think that is?

- What has been your vocational path? How did you end up in this profession? What is your specific job description right now?

- What is it like for you when you are unable to help people experience a "good death" or "healthy mourning"?

- As a grief caregiver, what is it like for you when you realize that we, as humans, never really completely "resolve" grief? How do you know that you are making a real difference in the lives of those you companion?

- What do you think some of the different motivations are for people who enter into this area of caregiving?

Did you learn anything about yourself in the process of answering the questions in this section? Just as there is no one right way of acting, thinking, speaking, or being in the helping relationship, there is no right background, set of current personal issues (or lack thereof), or motivations.

Every grief companion (and every mourner, for that matter) carries a unique pack of personal baggage to the trailhead. No one is immune from life losses and complex family histories. And our motivations are almost always multifaceted.

I will say, however, that for grief companions it is important not only to understand your own background, current personal issues, and motivations as much as possible, it is also important to have fully mourned and achieved reconciliation for your own past life losses before you enter into helping relationships. What's more, as new losses occur in your life, it is wise and appropriate for you to step out of your grief caregiving role for a time and/ or simultaneously seek individual counseling for your own grief even as you continue to companion others.

I realize that for grief companions, our own lives and losses, grief and mourning, can't and should not be fully compartmentalized from our work with our fellow human beings. In fact, the "self as instrument" philosophy celebrates the fact that we, too, are whole, complex human beings whose histories, individuality, and genuineness actually enhance our effectiveness at helping others. And it's often true that our wounds lead to our greatest strengths. I simply urge caution about the temptation or the potential pitfalls of using the companioning relationship to work through our own grief or carrying out our own agendas.

How can you tell if that's what you're doing? If you find yourself thinking a lot about your own losses or life during or after your companioning sessions, or if you notice that you're having a hard time being present to or nonjudgmental about certain thoughts and feelings the mourner expresses, take that as a sign that you need a professional sounding board—a colleague to discuss these issues with and give you feedback—or perhaps a professional grief companion to help you mourn any of your own grief you may be carrying.

Remember, you are standing at the trailhead, well prepared by the content of Part One, so that you can set off with the mourner to companion him on his unique grief journey. While of course you will learn from him and be changed by your interactions with him—and vice versa!—this journey is not about you. Consciously creating separate opportunities to mourn your own grief and work through your own issues will help you be the effective grief companion you want to be.

PART TWO:

THE PATH

NOW THAT YOU'VE ARRIVED AT THE TRAILHEAD WELL EQUIPPED TO HELP AND SUPPORT the mourner during her journey through the wilderness of grief, it's time to get going. Take a look down the path ahead of you. The trail is long and winding. The terrain is mountainous, and you can't yet see all the ups and downs, the twists and turns, to come.

"There are no wrong turnings— only paths we had not known we were meant to walk."

— GUY GAVRIEL KAY

But if you proceed firm in your understanding of the concepts covered in this section, you can walk with confidence that you can help the mourner meet most any challenge and keep lit the headlamp of hope, even during the darkest of moments.

MOURNER-CENTERED TALK THERAPY AS THE BEDROCK

As you walk alongside the mourner on her journey through grief, she will talk and you will listen—such a simple thing, really, but too often unavailable or unappreciated in our busy, distracted, grief-avoidant culture.

Talk therapy is not new, of course. The Austrian physician Josef Breuer was its first professional proponent, in the 1800s, and after him his protégé Sigmund Freud. They called it the "talking cure."

Then Carl Rogers came along. One of the most influential psychologists of the 20th century, he introduced the term "client-centered therapy" and championed its use. While Freud placed the therapist in the role of director and analyzer, Rogers believed that it is the person undergoing therapy who should lead the discussion, wherever she wanted it to go. In other words, the person receiving therapy—not the therapist—knows best about what ground needs to be covered, what is most pressing and important to discuss, and what meaning can be gleaned from the sessions. Rogers also thought that therapists should completely accept and support their clients, never judging, always empathetic. (Yet there will be appropriate times for supportive confrontation. More on that in a bit.)

"I've realized therapy is incredibly therapeutic."

— LISA SCHROEDER

"The word 'listen' contains the same letters as the word 'silent.'"

— ALFRED BRENDEL

I agree with Rogers, especially when it comes to companioning people in grief. The mourner and her highest-priority thoughts and feelings should guide every discussion. The grief companion should completely accept and support the mourner, never judging, always empathetic.

Since the days of Carl Rogers, a number of forms of talk therapy have been developed. Cognitive behavioral therapy (CBT), dialectic behavior therapy (DBT), interpersonal therapy (IPT), and classic psychotherapy are the main types in use today. Many mental health caregivers, perhaps you, use a combination of these techniques in working with the people in their care.

If you are trained in employing various types of talk therapy, by all means, keep them in your toolkit and draw upon them when you think they will help. But at the same time, it's essential to let the mourner choose at every fork in the road. Never forget that the mourner is the expert of his own grief journey, not you. What is most heavy on his mind and heart on any given day—or most welcome and in need of expression, such as new insights and gratitudes—should guide each session.

I also think that therapeutic techniques can often be tossed out the window in favor of good old-fashioned listening. If you are a lay or volunteer grief support person, you do not need to know how to use CBT, DBT, IPT, or any other therapeutic acronym to be an effective companion. Remember—the mourner is not ill. He does not need treatment or a "cure." He simply needs to express his inner thoughts and feelings as they arise and change over time. Simply talking them through in the presence of someone who deeply listens and accepts, week after week, is often enough.

> *"I have been sustained throughout my life by three saving graces—my family, my friends, and a faith in the power of resilience and hope. These graces have carried me through difficult times."*
> — ELIZABETH EDWARDS

NOT EVERYONE NEEDS FORMAL GRIEF COUNSELING

On a similar note, I want to be clear that not all mourners need grief counseling. Many will find various other ways to integrate significant loss into their lives. Yes, mourning is by definition "the shared, social response to loss," but mourners who have good support from family and friends and who typically embrace and express their thoughts and feelings will find that the normal adaptive grief process will unfold on its own. We as companions should avoid projecting that everyone needs some kind of professional intervention. The companioning model of grief care does advocate for a relational component of care, but it can often be supplied by trained laypeople or even friends and family members who are naturally good helpers.

Of course, some grievers will experience loss circumstances or other contributing factors (personality, loss history, cultural/religious background, a history of depression or mental illness, and more) that put them at risk for complicated grief. These people may well benefit from the help of clinicians who have an in-depth knowledge of complicated grief and mourning. Over the years I myself have developed a specialization in complicated mourning and provide supervision to other counselors who seek my mentorship.

CURING VERSUS CARING

"Cure" means to eradicate an illness, which, as we have already emphasized, grief is not. Care, on the other hand, is being present to, suffering with, and feeling with. Cure also means "to change." Caregivers often want to bring about change in people's lives, but cure can potentially damage if it does not grow out of care. Care is anchored in compassion and recognizes that this person who is hurting is my fellow human being, my brother or sister, mortal and vulnerable. And grief can never be eradicated, "gotten over," or "recovered from." It can only be experienced and, through active engagement, reconciled. We grief companions are caregivers, not cure-givers.

THE SIX NEEDS OF MOURNING AS THE TRAIL MARKERS

As you continue along the path with the mourner, walking and talking, you as the grief companion will know to look for certain touchstones, or trail markers. These are the mourning needs that each griever must meet on the journey to reconciliation.

I call these trail markers the six central needs of mourning. Those of you familiar with the literature on grief will note some similarities between the six needs of mourning and the observations of others in the field of grief care (Worden, Rando, Lindemann, Parkes, and Weiss).

THE SIX NEEDS OF MOURNING

1. Acknowledge the reality of the death

2. Feel the pain of the loss

3. Remember the person who died

4. Develop a new self-identity

5. Search for meaning

6. Receive ongoing support from others

It's helpful for both you and the mourner to be aware of these needs, because your mutual awareness can help build a participative, action-oriented understanding of grief and mourning in lieu of the common misperception that grief is something to be passively suffered or "treated away."

To that end, allow me to very briefly explain each of the six needs of mourning. For the grieving people in your care, you might recommend my book *Understanding Your Grief*. It includes an overview of the six needs of mourning as well as many other helpful discussions, affirmations, and tips about the normalcy and necessity of grief and mourning.

Please note that though the needs are numbered 1 through 6, they are not sequential in real life. Instead, mourners often encounter more than one at a time and in countless combinations. One need may be more pronounced this week, while another may be more pressing the next. What's more, the journey through the needs of mourning is recursive. It often loops back on itself, and mourners may feel as if they are getting lost, walking and walking in circles. This is normal.

"For in grief, nothing 'stays put.' One keeps on emerging from a phase, but it always recurs. Round and round. Everything repeats. Am I going in circles, or dare I hope I am on a spiral?"

— C.S. LEWIS

Similarly, you are probably aware of the "stages" of grief, popularized in 1969 by Elisabeth Kübler-Ross's landmark text *On Death and Dying*. In this book she lists the five stages of grief she saw terminally ill patients experience in the face of their own impending deaths: denial, anger, bargaining, depression, and acceptance. However, she never intended for her five stages to be applied to all grief or to be interpreted as a rigid, linear sequence to be followed by all mourners.

Your ability to create a holding environment—a safe place in the suspension of time—in which mourners feel welcome to dose themselves with the following mourning needs is a large part of the grief companion's job description.

Mourning need 1: *Acknowledge the reality of the death*

This need of mourning involves gently confronting the reality that someone the mourner has cared about—given love to and received love from—has died. Whether the death was sudden or anticipated, fully acknowledging the reality may occur over weeks, months, and sometimes even years. As humans, we can know something in our heads (the cognitive reality) but not in our hearts (the affective reality).

One moment the reality of the loss may be tolerable to the mourner; another moment it may be unbearable. As a grief companion, your role is to be patient and gentle as the mourner naturally visits and revisits this need. You should not force or direct but instead trust that the mourner will embrace the reality in doses over time. In the safety of your attentive acceptance, he can and will work on this difficult need.

Mourning need 2: *Feel the pain of the loss*

As I've said, to be "bereaved" literally means "to be torn apart." When a person is torn apart by loss, it hurts not only emotionally but also physically, cognitively, socially, and spiritually. And embracing the hurt—even wallowing in it at times—is essential to healing.

> *"Your pain is the breaking of the shell that encloses your understanding."*
> — KAHLIL GIBRAN

Yet the medical model of grief care too often implies that hurting is bad or unnecessary. Emotional and spiritual pain should be treated away as quickly as possible, the thinking goes. Also having been influenced by our mourning-avoidant culture, mourners themselves will commonly come to you in the hopes that you will make the pain go away.

Learning how to be present to pain without trying to soothe it away is one of the grief companion's greatest challenges. The helping skills we will soon discuss are your most important tools for empathetically bearing witness to pain.

Mourning need 3: *Remember the person who died*

This need is anchored in affirming and subtly encouraging the mourner to pursue a relationship of memory with the person who died. While many people in the mourner's life may tell her that she needs to "move on" and "let go," the truth is that she needs to convert her relationship with the person who died from one of presence to one of memory.

As grief companion your role is to help the mourner feel affirmed in remembering. Memories in all forms—good, bad, and indifferent; dreams reflecting the significance of the relationship; and objects linking the mourner to the person who died (such as photos, souvenirs, clothing, etc.)—are helpful in meeting this need and give testimony to a kind of transformed but continued relationship.

Intently attending to the mourner's memory-sharing and storytelling, with genuine interest and compassion, is one of your most essential tasks as a grief companion. The more effective your helping skills, the more effective you will be as a memory receiver.

Mourning need 4: *Develop a new self-identity*

The mourner must evolve a new self-identity based on a life without the physical presence of the person who died—and all the interconnected relationship cues and structure that person made possible.

Part of every human being's self-identity comes from the relationships she has with others. The mourner may have gone from being a "wife" or "husband" to a "widow" or "widower." Or she may have lost her parent, best friend, or child. Each of these relationships connected her in countless ways both to her day-to-day life and to her place in her family and community. Now there's a gaping hole in the constellation of her life.

> *"We are all butterflies.*
> *Earth is our chrysalis."*
> — LEEANN TAYLOR

Readjusting the constellation so that it finds a new wholeness is part of her journey. This is very hard work and can leave the mourner feeling drained of emotional, physical, and spiritual energy.

As always, your self is an instrument that compassionately affirms and bears witness to the mourner's encounters with this mourning need yet refrains from trying to direct or find answers to the struggle.

Mourning need 5: *Search for meaning*

When someone loved dies, the mourner naturally questions the meaning and purpose of life. He may question his worldview and explore religious and spiritual values and faith as he works on this need. He will often ask "why?" and "how?" questions: "Why did this happen now, in this way?" "How will I go on living?" The "why?" questions often precede the "how?" questions in this unfolding process.

The mourner's search for meaning and reasons to go on living is a vital part of grief work. For the grief companion, enabling this natural and necessary search for meaning involves creating a safe place in which the mourner feels invited to ask such questions. Resisting the urge to offer answers is equally essential.

In fact, for the mourner the very key to meeting this need is the often long, looping, and illogical path she will take to find her own answers. You facilitate the meeting of the need by bearing witness and using your helping skills judiciously.

> "Questions can be like a lever you use to pry open the stuck lid of a paint can."
>
> — FRAN PEAVEY

A caveat: If you are asked directly by the mourner what *you* believe about the meaning of life and death, the afterlife, spiritual experiences, etc., you should, of course, answer honestly. After all, all relationships are by definition reciprocal, and the trust you are building with the mourner requires some degree of give-and-take. However, I encourage you to answer such questions briefly and in service of the mourner, quickly returning the focus to his unique journey after you share.

Mourning need 6: *Receive ongoing support from others*

Grievers need help and encouragement to mourn. You understand this! That's why you're reading this book! From the bottom of my heart, I thank you for your efforts to help people in grief. I truly believe there is no higher calling in life.

If you are new to grief companioning, what you may not yet realize is that because mourning is a dosed process that unfolds over time, the mourner will need support for months and even years after the death. Unfortunately, because our society places so much emphasis on returning to "normal" within a short period of time, many grieving people are abandoned by their friends and family members shortly after the funeral.

When possible, an essential ingredient of your companioning role is to support the mourner not only in the period of acute grief, but over the long-term. To heal, grief requires not only active engagement with the six needs of mourning but also a period of convalescence—a very slow, gradual return to health after an injury. During your sessions with the mourner, you can affirm that grief is often a lengthy journey and that no matter how many weeks or months your companioning relationship continues (it may be restricted by insurance limits or other practicalities), he should continue to heed his instinct to seek out the support of others.

THE HELPING SKILLS AS THE TOOLS

In many ways, learning specific helping skills is like learning to paint on canvas. In the beginning, you're learning how to hold the brush, mix the paint, and create various brushstrokes. Only after much practice will you be ready to transcend the tools and techniques and create real art. Similarly, only after you as a grief

---

"The act of compassion begins with full attention, just as rapport does. You have to really see the person. If you see the person, then naturally, empathy arises. If you tune into the other person, you feel with them. If empathy arises, and if that person is in dire need, then empathic concern can come. You want to help them, and then that begins a compassionate act. So I'd say that compassion begins with attention."

—DANIEL GOLEMAN

---

companion have learned and practiced your helping skills will you begin to really understand what it means to transcend the technique and develop "the art of helping."

I also believe that helping our fellow human beings during times of crisis is every bit as much an "art" as it is a "science." Interpersonal skills are more than a collection of techniques. Helping others is a demanding, intimate experience that requires energy, focus, and a desire to understand not only other people, but also yourself.

THREE LEVELS OF COMMUNICATION

Companion-mourner communication can be seen as an exchange between two people. And actually, three very different, yet interdependent, levels of communication exist:

1. the exchange of information
2. the exchange of emotion
3. the exchange of meaning

The **exchange of information** involves the interaction of the companion and the mourner as the companion seeks to understand the 5 Ws: who, what, why, where, when, and also how. Who are you? Tell me about yourself. Who died? What happened? Why, where, and when did it happen? How did it happen? While this process may seem simple, this exchange is complicated by the reality that humans do not give and receive information passively. The emotional state of each person in the interaction, as well as how each person feels about the other person, affects the nature of the interaction. So, it's never as simple as asking questions and getting answers. Even in early conversations, when it seems like mostly introductions are taking place, communication is actually happening on many levels.

Of course, an **exchange of emotion** also occurs between companion and mourner. You are working with grieving people who will be very sensitive to your capacity to empathize and "be with" them. When grief companions are effective at using interpersonal skills, which is the topic of this book, this allows the mourner to appropriately focus on her thoughts and feelings. Poor interpersonal skills on the part of the companion force the mourner to focus on the companion—Why is he not listening carefully? My honesty is making him uncomfortable!

Finally, over time an **exchange of meaning** occurs. Once the informational phase is taken care of and the acute thoughts and feelings are expressed and fully explored, meaning begins to build in the companion-mourner interaction.

THE ROLE OF EMPATHY

As a grief caregiver, you may know that many nonprofessional people use the words "sympathy" and "empathy" interchangeably. Yet there is an important difference between the two—and you will leverage this difference to make yourself a better helper.

When you are sympathetic to someone else, you are noticing and feeling concern for his circumstances, usually at a distance. You're "feeling sorry" for him. You are feeling "pity" for him. You are looking at his situation from the outside, and you are acknowledging the distress passively. You may be offering a simple solution, platitude, or distraction. Sometimes sympathy also includes a touch (or a heavy dose) of judgment or superiority. Sympathy is "feeling for" someone else.

For professional caregivers, sympathy is often a protective response to grief overload (too many grieving people with overwhelming loss experiences need help) and/or a professional distancing learned through medical-model training and organizational culture and requirements (diagnostic codes, treatment language, etc.).

More destructive even than sympathy is identification. This attitude is conveyed by those who submerge themselves with the griever and try to take on their feelings for them. These are people who make assumptions like, "I know just how you feel." The last person the griever feels safe with is one who conveys this attitude of over-identification.

> *"Empathy is full presence to what's alive in the other person at this moment."*
>
> — JOHN CUNNINGHAM

Empathy, on the other hand, is about making an emotional connection. It is a more active process—one in which you try to understand and feel the other person's experience from the inside out rather than imposing meaning from the outside in. You are not judging the person or the circumstances. You are not offering simple solutions. Instead, you are making yourself vulnerable to the person's ever-changing thoughts, feelings, and circumstances by looking for connections to similar thoughts, feelings, and circumstances inside you. You are being present and allowing yourself to be taught by the other person. Empathy is "feeling with" someone else.

From a grief caregiving standpoint, empathy normalizes. It welcomes. It creates a safe space. It builds the relationship between caregiver and griever. It assumes nothing but instead creates an opening for the griever to teach the caregiver what the experience is like for him.

On the journey through grief, active empathy is about exploration. The companion is trying to grasp what it is like inside the soul—the life force—of the griever. Empathetic responsiveness requires the ability to go deeper than the surface and to become involved in the mourner's feeling world—but always with an "as if" quality of taking another's role without personally experiencing what the other person experiences. What is the inner flavor and what are the unique meanings that the person's experience has for him? What is it that she is trying to express but can't quite say in words?

Empathy is communicated when you, the companion, respond at the emotional, feeling level of the mourner. You reach the mourner where he is, being careful not to bring judgment or a need to get him to "let go" and "move on." This dependable quality of empathy is what seems to free the mourner to open his heart and mourn from the inside out. You will know you are actively empathizing when the mourner trusts you and feels you truly understand.

> *"If we share our story with someone who responds with empathy and understanding, shame can't survive."*
>
> — BRENÉ BROWN

Your capacity to convey active empathy has a number of benefits for the mourner. Among them are:

- Empathetic communication is a foundation upon which you establish a companioning relationship with the mourner.

- The mourner who feels empathetically understood and not judged is more likely to risk sharing deep, soul-based encounters with grief.

- The mourner's experience of your genuine effort and commitment to understand creates a trusting, low-threat environment that may override any tendencies the mourner may have for self-protection and isolation.

- The communication of empathy encourages the mourner to self-explore, a prerequisite for compassionate self-understanding and, eventually, movement toward reconciliation.

Active empathy is the most essential tool for the grief companion as you walk alongside the mourner on her journey through grief. You communicate your empathy through your use of the helping skills, which are up next.

COMPASSIONATE PRESENCE

In the field of psychology, study after study has shown that what facilitates positive change and growth in counseling clients is the relationship formed with the caregiver. The helping skills contribute to this relationship, of course, but they do not form the totality of the relationship.

For grief companions, the relationship with mourners is built upon the idea of "compassionate presence." Your compassionate presence is how you are able to "be with" mourners and stands in contrast to the medical model's focus on how to "do something" for patients or clients.

Compassionately being with mourners means being fully present and actively and empathetically listening. It means creating a "holding environment"—a safe place and a cleaned-out heart that stand by ready to hospitably bear witness to and accommodate whatever the mourner thinks and feels.

The idea of compassionate presence ties into the self-as-instrument philosophy we discussed earlier. When you bring your compassionate presence to the helping relationship, you are doing so with an awareness that you are an instrument on the journey to healing.

ATTENDING (OR ACTIVE LISTENING)

In interpersonal interactions, attending means fully and actively listening with the intent not only to cognitively understand everything that is being said, but also to *feel* what is being said. It means giving your undivided attention and focus. It means paying attention to both verbal and nonverbal cues. And it also means communicating your high degree of attention and focus back to the other person.

As a grief companion, you may find that you are one of the few people who actually listen to grieving people. Even when mourners are surrounded by family and friends, they are often not really listened to.

The renowned Buddhist monk and teacher Thich Nhat Hanh calls it "deep listening." Here's what he says about it:

"Deep listening is the kind of listening that can help relieve the suffering of the other person. You can call it compassionate listening. You listen with only one purpose: to help him or her empty his heart. And if you remember that you are helping him or her to suffer less, and then

> *"Listening is a magnetic and strange thing, a creative force. The friends who listen to us are the ones we move toward. When we are listened to, it creates us, makes us unfold and expand."*
> — KARL A. MENNINGER

even if he says things full of wrong perceptions, full of bitterness, you are still capable to listen with compassion. One hour like that can bring transformation and healing."

Yes, even one single hour of being truly listened to can make a world of difference.

Personal qualities of an effective listener:

- **Desire.** Perhaps the single most important characteristic of the good listener is desire. While this sounds simplistic, you need to *want* to listen. If you do not want to listen, chances are you will not really listen. What's more, people can detect a superficial desire to listen.

- **Commitment.** An effective listener not only needs to have a general desire to listen but also needs to have a commitment to the task of listening. To be committed means to be responsible. If you are unable to talk at a particular time, be honest.

> *"Most people do not listen with the intent to understand; they listen with the intent to reply."*
> — STEPHEN R. COVEY

Share your desire to talk and arrange for another time.

- **Patience.** Good listeners are patient. They allow the sharing and conversation to unfold naturally without feeling the need to hurry it along or "cut to the chase."

A NOTE ABOUT SILENCE

Effective grief companions understand that sometimes attending to and sitting with silence is the best way to help someone. You do not have to— nor should you try to—fill every gap in the conversation. There is a time for speaking, and there is a time for silence. Sometimes mourners need a moment to collect their thoughts or process a new insight. Sometimes they simply need to cry or even to feel. Sometimes they don't know what to say, and if you rush in too soon or too often with leading questions or ideas, you will end up leading their mourning.

What's more, silence is sacred. When you remain quiet, you sustain an open heart and a gentle spirit. Consciously hush yourself and place trust in the peace you help initiate. Become fully present to another human being who doesn't really need your words but values your soulful presence.

Yes, it can be uncomfortable to sit with silence, but learning the art of when to allow silence to reign is part of your task in honing your fundamental counseling skills. Silence itself can speak volumes if you know how to witness it. As Henry David Thoreau said, "The tragedy begins not when there is misunderstanding about words, but when silence is not understood."

LISTENING BEHAVIORS

Technically speaking, you listen with your ears, which convey the sounds to your brain. But in human terms you listen with your entire body, and you communicate your active, empathetic listening back to the speaker through a variety of actions and behaviors.

I'm sure you've heard it said that communication is 60 percent body language, 30 percent tone, and 10 percent words. Let's talk about that critical 60 percent.

"Perhaps the most important thing we bring to another person is the silence in us, not the sort of silence that is filled with unspoken criticism or hard withdrawal. The sort of silence that is a place of refuge, of rest, of acceptance of someone as they are. We are all hungry for this other silence. It is hard to find. In its presence we can remember something beyond the moment, a strength on which to build a life. Silence is a place of great power and healing."

— RACHEL NAOMI REMEN

NONVERBAL COMMUNICATION

Eye contact

Perhaps the most effective way of connecting with people, especially when they are emotional, is with eye contact. It was Shakespeare who said that the eyes are the windows to the soul.

Indeed, looking into the eyes of someone who is feeling pain will tell you much of what you need to know.

Practice looking at the mourner's eyes as she speaks and also when she is silent. Do not maintain a fixed stare, for that can feel aggressive or rude, but do maintain eye contact much of the time. Try looking at one of the mourner's eyes for a few seconds, then looking at the other eye for a few seconds, then looking at his hair or chin for a few seconds. This rotation usually works to help him feel well attended to but not creepily stared at. As your relationship grows stronger, you will find that you can hold the mourner's gaze longer and more often.

> *"This is the problem with dealing with someone who is actually a good listener. They don't jump in on your sentences, saving you from actually finishing them, or talk over you, allowing what you do manage to get out to be lost or altered in transit. Instead, they wait, so you have to keep going."*
>
> — SARAH DESSEN

Also refrain from "shifty" eye contact. Eyes that dart around and don't settle on anything for more than a second or so are perceived as communicating dishonesty or untrustworthiness.

You may have noticed that people in distress, including mourners, may seek less eye contact. If they are sharing something that is difficult for them, they may look down or away. In fact, it's normal for people who are embarrassed, sad, or trying to articulate deeply internal emotions or memories to direct their gaze away from the person they are talking to.

When the mourner breaks eye contact, you will often want to keep

"When I ask you to listen to me and you start giving me advice, you have not done what I asked.

"When I ask you to listen to me and you are telling me why I shouldn't feel that way, you are trampling on my feelings.

"When I ask you to listen to me and you feel you have to do something to solve my problems, you have failed me, strange as that may seem.

"Perhaps that's why prayer works for some people. Because God is mute and he doesn't offer advice or try to fix things. He just listens and trusts you to work it for yourself. So please, just listen and hear me. And if you want to talk, wait a few minutes for your turn and I promise I'll listen to you."

— AUTHOR UNKNOWN

looking at her eyes as she speaks or sits in silence. But sometimes you will want to be respectful of her need to take a break from being "looked at." Studies have also shown that women are comfortable with more face-to-face eye contact than are men, who are more likely to speak to each other when they are positioned side-by-side.

Figuring out what is just the right amount of eye contact for each unique mourner can be tricky, but the more you practice your fundamental counseling skills, the better you will get at instinctively knowing how much and when to use the power of gaze.

Posture
Every moment of every day, we communicate a great deal by how we stand, sit, and move. Take a moment right now to

become aware of your posture and what it might communicate to someone entering the room. When you are involved in a helping relationship, your posture can convey an interest and readiness to assist—or it can communicate disinterest, distraction, or even defensiveness.

A sense of relaxation in your posture is also important. When we are nervous or anxious, our posture naturally grows more stiff. Our muscles tense, as if we might take off at any moment. This is part of our bodies' subconscious, fear-based fight-or-flight mechanism.

When we are relaxed, on the other hand, our muscles relax, our posture relaxes, and our stance (standing or seated) opens up a bit. Closed posture, on the other hand, which includes crossed arms, crossed legs, and/or body angled away from the mourner, literally places a barrier between you and the mourner.

Take care not to slouch, though. Slouching says, "I'm bored or overly casual." Pretend that a helium balloon is tied to the top of your head and is pulling you upward. Keep your feet on the floor. Don't fidget.

Interest in also communicated by leaning your upper body toward the other person just a bit. Leaning away is generally a distancing posture.

Try practicing your companioning posture in front of a full-length mirror. Rope someone into helping you practice, and set up two chairs where you can see your whole body in the mirror. Engage in a conversation with the other person, but before you begin, set your phone to sound a tone every couple of minutes. When you hear the tone, look over at the mirror and notice your posture. What does your posture communicate? Is it an appropriately, actively-empathetic listening posture? Adjust your posture if needed and continue the conversation. When the alarm sounds again, recheck your posture and readjust. This exercise will help you learn what your normal, unconscious posture looks like and make a plan, if needed, to improve it.

Physical distance

The amount of distance you place between yourself and the mourner as the two of you converse affects his perception of your capacity to care and be helpful. At times, an appropriate behavior is to move in very close as you reach out to comfort. Use the other person's reaction as a guide. If she pulls away, take that as an indication that you are too close.

I've found that most people are comfortable at a distance of about three feet away. Exactly how close you sit, and whether you sit straight across from the mourner or at a slight angle to the side, depends on your personal style as well as the unique personality of the mourner.

The more helping experience you gain, the more you will learn to read the mourner's body language, which in turn will help you determine how far away and where to sit as well as how much eye contact to maintain and other behaviors. If the mourner crosses his arms, leans away, turns to the side, or looks away frequently, you can assume that he needs a little more physical distance and autonomy and may need more time to develop trust in your relationship.

Facial expression

The expression on your face should match, as closely as possible, the emotional tone of the mood you are hearing and discerning from the mourner. In human beings "mirroring" is an instinctive behavior that expresses empathy and builds relationships.

While facial expression is fairly instinctive, especially in people with a high capacity for empathy, sometimes people's facial expressions do not match up well with what they are feeling inside. In particular, our "resting faces"—what we look like when we are in a neutral waiting or observing state—sometimes convey emotions we aren't actually feeling and don't intend to convey.

> *"Few realize how loud their expressions really are. Be kind with what you wordlessly say."*
>
> — RICHELLE E. GOODRICH

If your resting face expresses something other than what you intend, you may be able to work on adjusting it a bit for your companioning sessions. Look in the mirror and try to look concerned. Now try to look welcoming. Now try to look focused. See how you subtly move your facial muscles as you cycle through these expressions? With practice, you can fine-tune your companioning resting face so that it feels and looks natural and communicates active empathy. Ask a friend to read your expressions and help you make adjustments.

And don't forget to smile whenever appropriate!

Gestures

Gestures are the final form of body language that convey active listening and empathy. Your gestures should be natural and should not interfere with your intended communication.

Take care not to fidget. Don't click your pen, jiggle your legs, play with your hair, or engage in any other repetitive physical behaviors. While these may be natural "tics" for you—movements that might actually help you concentrate—they are not appropriate for a grief companion because they are distracting and put attention on you rather than the mourner.

If you move too quickly, this can also be unnerving to the mourner. Be careful not to rush to your chair, shake hands too energetically, or gesture too wildly. Both speed and large motions are disconcerting. They compete for attention and run counter to the mourner's need to slow down, look inward, and feel safe in expressing her thoughts and feelings.

This depends on your personal style, but helpful gestures often include some head nodding, although not too much, and, when your hands aren't still in your lap, open, lifted palms. Conversely, hidden hands or hands that don't move can convey dishonesty or apathy.

> *"He had the look of one who had drunk the cup of life and found a dead beetle at the bottom."*
>
> — P.G. WODEHOUSE

Setting

At times you will have little, if any, control over the setting in which you companion your grieving fellow human beings. But when you do, consider the following suggestions:

- *Seek solitude.* Find a space in which you can be alone with the mourner, without any outside distractions.

- *Enforce quiet.* Close the door, turn off music and phones, and let the only sounds be that of you and the mourner communicating.

- *Seat optimally.* Place chairs face to face or at a slight angle, about three feet apart. I sometimes sit beside the mourner, both of us facing the same direction, when I know they are searching for meaning or doing "why?" work. Choose chairs that will be comfortable for people of various body shapes and sizes to sit in for a full hour. Armchairs are usually more comfortable than chairs without arms. Try not to put a desk, table, or any other barrier between you and the mourner.

- *Consider décor.* If possible, consider the aesthetics of the space in which you will be meeting. Colors, clutter, materials, and cleanliness all matter. At a minimum, clear away clutter and make sure the room is clean and lit well—not too bright but not too dark, either. Lighting from table or floor lamps is generally more welcoming than that from overhead commercial fixtures.

SOLER POWER

Have you heard the acronym SOLER to describe effective counseling body language, devised in 1975 by therapist Gerard Egan?

S	Sit straight.
O	Open posture.
L	Lean forward.
E	Eye contact.
R	Relax.

SOLER is a helpful mnemonic you can run through silently in your mind every time you sit down for a companioning session.

Level of energy

This element of nonverbal communication mostly has to do with staying power. Are you remaining alert and attentive throughout your conversation with the mourner? Or do you find your mind wandering and your energy flagging? If the latter, you may need to work on your companioning endurance.

Focusing entirely and empathetically on another human being's experience for a long period of time can be draining. Limiting each helping session to an hour is usually a good idea. If you find yourself losing concentration, getting sleepy, feeling the need to move around, or even getting irritated—and it's been more than an hour—it's time to gracefully move toward wrapping up the day's interaction.

Physical appearance

Whether you realize it or not, your physical appearance communicates respect or disrespect to those you are working so hard to help. Poor grooming and hygiene as well as clothing that is ill-fitting, distasteful, scanty, or in bad condition can indicate to the mourner that you do not take your helping role seriously. Good grooming and hygiene, on the other hand, as well as casual, professional dress, convey that you believe the time you spend with mourners is important.

In all of our counseling interactions, we as grief companions want mourners to feel welcome, safe, understood, and yes, attended to. Our physical appearance is one factor that can make our fellow human beings feel unwelcome, unattended, and sometimes even a bit unsafe (because extremely poor physical care is so outside social norms).

Please understand that I am definitely NOT saying you need to conform to any societal conventions of attractiveness to be a good grief companion. Attractiveness is unimportant; it only matters that you present your physical self professionally and respectfully (even if you are a volunteer or lay helper). Beyond that, it's all about genuine empathy and companioning skills.

Listening Behaviors and Rapport

In your interactions with mourners, you will be working toward building the sometimes elusive quality of rapport. From the French word of the same spelling, which means "harmony or agreement," rapport with the grieving people you are working to support is mostly built nonverbally. When you effectively use all of the active listening skills and considerations we have been reviewing so far, you will generally enjoy good rapport with mourners. Yes, verbal skills and factors contribute to rapport as well, such as the effective use of humor, but in the grief companioning relationship, rapport is mostly a bond built while the mourner speaks and you listen.

As a species, we are highly attuned to nonverbal communication. We trust others based more on their body language and tone of voice than on the content of their spoken language, in fact. While you might think that the nonverbal components of your companioning skills are wholly instinctual or set in stone, it's not true. You developed your current nonverbal interpersonal behaviors over all the years you've been alive. You learned them from your parents, siblings, and other family members as well as close friends. They changed as you got older. Your working life continued to mold them. And now you have the opportunity to refine them yet again—this time on purpose—to help you become a more effective grief companion.

> *"People don't care how much you know until they know how much you care."*
> —JOHN C. MAXWELL

IS IT MY JOB TO MAKE THE MOURNER FEEL BETTER?

When I was first being trained as a counselor, I thought that was my job. After all, I pondered, isn't that why people come in for counseling? With time, experience, and good supervision, I began to realize my role was not to take the pain of grief away but instead to be present to it. I remember my mentor, Dr. Ken Dimick, saying to me, "Always start with your mouth closed and your ears open." Excellent attending/listening skills are the essence of being fully present to the mourner. My mantra is: "Enter into the pain; do not take it away. I am responsible *to* this person, not *for* this person."

Your capacity to provide your full attention and compassionate presence to the mourner is the most important gift you can bring to the helping relationship.

VERBAL COMMUNICATION SKILLS

Now let's take a look at the language skills you use to help people in mourning. So far we've emphasized talk therapy—in which the mourner talks and you listen—and we've covered nonverbal attending or active listening skills. But sometimes you as a grief companion do need to talk, of course. Knowing when and how to most effectively use your powers of speech will help you be the best grief companion you can be.

Before we dive into the verbal companioning skills, here are two verbal fine-tuning tips to always keep in mind:

- Tone of Voice
  Tone of voice is one of the most important attending skills to master. As Maya Angelou famously said, "People will forget what you said, people will forget what you did, but people will never forget how you made them feel."

  An empathetic tone is gentle, lilting, and usually at the lower end of your register. Over my many years as a grief companion, I've also found that quiet is often more effective than loud or even normal speaking volume.

- Rate of Speech
  If you talk too quickly, you will sound impatient. If you talk too

slowly, you may communicate uncertainty or boredom. Try speaking at a natural pace, but if in doubt, slow it down just a hair.

Paraphrasing

Paraphrasing is a skill that allows you to affirm what the mourner is trying to communicate to you, making her feel listened to and understood. This skill is when you as the caregiver extract the essence of what the mourner says to you and give it back to her in fewer words. Hearing a paraphrase of her thoughts and feelings often helps the mourner sharpen her own understanding of those thoughts and feelings. This skill also allows the mourner an opportunity to clarify or expand on what she thinks and feels.

Here are some examples of paraphrasing:

MOURNER:
"I'm just so tired all the time. I don't want to get off the couch. I have zero energy for anything I'm supposed to be doing."

GRIEF COMPANION'S PARAPHRASE:
"You're feeling really fatigued and low energy most days."

MOURNER:
"I'm so mad at him for not buckling his seatbelt and driving recklessly. He should have been more careful! His carelessness will affect me and our whole family for the rest of our lives!"

GRIEF COMPANION'S PARAPHRASE:
"You're angry at him for not being more careful."

MOURNER:
"Everywhere I go, I keep expecting to see Gina. Like she's going to walk up to me as if nothing's happened. Or she's going to say, 'Surprise! Just kidding! I'm still here!' I really can't get my mind around the fact that she's gone."

GRIEF COMPANION'S PARAPHRASE:

"Sounds like it is hard to believe Gina is not going to walk through the door."

MOURNER:

"What am I supposed to believe? Am I supposed to think he's in some wonderful place called heaven right now? Or should I just be realistic and assume he's dead and gone and that's it?"

GRIEF COMPANION'S PARAPHRASE:

"It sounds like you're struggling with whether you believe there's an afterlife or not."

As you learn to refine your paraphrasing skills, simply ask yourself, "What is this person saying and feeling?" Then, when a natural break occurs in the interaction, offer your paraphrase. As you develop this skill, you will discover that the person you are attending to will often confirm the accuracy of your paraphrase either verbally or nonverbally.

When you are paraphrasing, you may find yourself tempted to add onto or further develop the mourner's message. Resist this urge. A real difference exists between paraphrasing and interpreting. If you find yourself embellishing or developing the mourner's basic message, odds are you have moved in the direction of projecting your own thoughts into the interaction. This often takes the focus off the person you are helping and puts it on you.

Here are some examples of embellishing or projection:

MOURNER:

"I'm just so tired all the time. I don't want to get off the couch. I have zero energy for anything I'm supposed to be doing."

GRIEF COMPANION'S EMBELLISHMENT (NOT PARAPHRASE):

"You're often tired and need help identifying ways to get more energy. Have you tried walking a little every day?"

MOURNER:

"I'm so mad at him for not buckling his seatbelt and driving recklessly. He should have been more careful! His carelessness will affect me and our whole family for the rest of our lives!"

GRIEF COMPANION'S EMBELLISHMENT (NOT PARAPHRASE):

"You're angry at him and wish you could tell him about the damage his actions caused."

MOURNER:

"Everywhere I go, I keep expecting to see Gina. Like she's going to walk up to me as if nothing's happened. Or she's going to say, 'Surprise! Just kidding! I'm still here!' I really can't get my mind around the fact that she's gone."

GRIEF COMPANION'S EMBELLISHMENT (NOT PARAPHRASE):

"Yes, it's common for mourners to think they see the person who died. I've had that happen to me, actually."

Over time you will discover that good paraphrasing dramatically enhances your ability to listen. To use this skill effectively, you must want to understand the person, communicate meaningfully, and relate with acceptance and trust. Your efforts to learn this and the other skills outlined in this text are evidence of your commitment to enhance your helpfulness as a grief companion.

A FEW WORDS ON PATIENCE

Effective grief companions understand that it is the mourners in their care—not them—who set the pace on the journey through grief. And to both you and the mourner, this pace can sometimes feel maddeningly slow, circuitous, and even stalled altogether.

Active mourning does create movement (we'll talk more about that on page 92), but the movement may be naturally slow at times. When this happens, you must take care not to rush in to lead the mourner toward an "aha!" or in a direction of your choosing.

Grief takes as long as it takes, and with active mourning, it can and will soften over time. But there are no rewards for speed. Your role is to empathetically listen and use the helping skills we are reviewing in this book to facilitate the mourner's active exploration of his wilderness—even when that exploration seems to involve going nowhere.

> *"Make your ego porous.*
> *Will is of little importance,*
> *complaining is nothing,*
> *fame is nothing. Openness,*
> *patience, receptivity,*
> *solitude is everything."*
> — RAINER MARIA RILKE

As you companion, try to remember Tenet 8 of my principles of grief companioning, which says that companioning is about being still—not about frantic movement forward. If and when you feel a surge of impatience or the need to lead, be still. Breathe slowly and deeply, and regard the mourner with empathy. Sit with her in her lostness while you exude hope and faith that she will regain her footing.

I've heard many caregivers say that patience is the most challenging companioning quality to develop. I understand the impulse to want to "fix" and "solve," but truly, healing in grief does not work that way. Healing unfolds from the inside out. Your patience in bearing witness to this unfolding is far more transformative than any shortcuts you could offer.

Clarifying

When people are experiencing grief, communicating clearly becomes naturally difficult. Shock and disorientation can make it hard to get thoughts and feelings to flow well. The grief companion who learns to clarify skillfully can work to better understand the mourner as well as help the mourner better understand herself.

Clarifying is used to bring any vague or confusing statements into sharper focus. Again, be careful not to over-interpret or embellish. Instead, focus solely on clarifying. Be sure to state your clarifying remarks in terms of your own feelings of confusion, thereby avoiding any implications of criticism.

"It's a lack of clarity that creates chaos and frustration. Those emotions are poison to any living goal."

— STEVE MARABOLI

"If we have no peace, it is because we have forgotten that we belong to each other."

— MOTHER TERESA

Remember that people in grief often naturally feel cognitively disorganized and disoriented. Also keep in mind that the confusion might occasionally, at least in part, be due to your own inattention to what the person has just said. You can simply ask the mourner to restate what was said, ask for an example, or offer a paraphrase and confirmation.

Here are some examples of clarifying statements:

After a period of confusing discussion, you might say...

"I'm confused. Let me try to state what I think you were trying to help me understand." (followed by a tentative paraphrase)
or

"I'm not sure I understand. Maybe we can go over that again."

or

"I'm lost. Can you tell me more?"

USING YOUR HELPING SKILLS TO FACILITATE SUPPORT GROUPS

In North America today, many mourners find companionship in the form of grief support groups. The worth of these programs certainly does not emanate from empirically supported treatments but from something much more simple (yet powerful): the telling of stories. The meetings are anchored in honoring each member's stories of grief and supporting each other's need to authentically mourn. No effort is made to interpret or analyze. The group affirms the storyteller for the courage to express the raw wounds that often accompany loss. The stories speak the truth. The stories create hope. The stories create healing.

Effective leaders of such groups come to recognize that their role is not so much about group counseling techniques as it is about creating "sacred space" in the group so that each person's story can be non-judgmentally received. Effective grief group leadership is a humble yet demanding role of creating this space in ways that members can express their wounds in the body of community. The very experience of telling one's story in the common bond of the group contradicts the isolation and shame that characterizes so many people's lives in a mourning-avoidant culture. And, because stories of love and loss take time, patience, and unconditional love, they serve as powerful antidotes to a modern society that is all too often preoccupied with getting people to "let go" and "move on."

Notice how I said "demanding"? That's because facilitating a grief support group means using all of your helping skills with multiple people at the same time. It also means stepping in to ensure effective communication among members. So while the support group is not about or for you and should not be used as an arena in which to over-use your counseling techniques and expertise, the group will very much rely on your skillful communication and facilitation to make sure that everyone has a chance to speak if they would like, feels safe and understood, feels protected from members who might be hurtful or judgmental, and is given the opportunity to cover new ground and proceed at a pace that works for them.

A challenging situation indeed! If you are interested in learning to facilitate grief support groups or enhancing your group helping skills if you are already facilitating, I encourage you to attend my Support Group Facilitator Training, held every other year in Fort Collins, Colorado.

> *"People help you, or you help them, and when we offer or receive help, we take in each other. And then we are saved."*
>
> — ANNE LAMOTT

Perception Checking

When people are grieving, miscommunication is common. Perception checking is a skill every grief companion should work to refine. Having the ability to ask supportively for feedback about your understanding of what is said will dramatically increase your companioning skills overall.

Like paraphrasing, perception checking tries to restate what the mourner just said, but in a more tentative way. In fact, it's kind of a cross between paraphrasing and clarifying.

When you are in the position of helping others, you are responsible for ensuring clear communication. You don't want to be stuck with misunderstanding something important. Perception checking is a means of ensuring accurate understanding. The mourner you are assisting will appreciate your efforts to be certain that you are understanding one another.

Here are some examples of perception-checking questions:

"You expressed some doubt about your father's ability to be

supportive of you. **Did I hear you correctly?**" (Asking "Did I hear you correctly?" allows the person you are helping to clarify any confusion in your understanding.)

"I want to check in with you about what I think I heard you say. You said you would like to have a memorial service, but you are not sure when would be the best time?" (Stating "I want to check in with you about what I think I heard you say" helps the person realize that you want to check on your understanding.)

> *"I know you believe what you think I said, but I'm not sure that what you heard is what I really meant to say."*
>
> — AUTHOR UNKNOWN

"While you want to go to the cemetery next week, you think it's important for you to go alone. **Is that right?**" (Asking "Is that right?" allows the person you are helping to clear up any confusion in your understanding.)

THE POWER OF STORY

When you think about it, the foundation of grief companioning mostly involves listening and bearing witness to the mourner's stories of love and loss. Far from child's play, such storytelling is powerful because it gives shape and meaning to the mourner's experiences.

In telling their stories of love and loss, mourners can

- search for wholeness among their fractured parts.
- come to know who they are in new and unexpected ways.
- explore their past and come to a more profound understanding of their origins and future directions.
- explain their view of the world and come to understand who they are.
- explore how love experienced and love lost have influenced their time on earth.

- discover that a life without story is like a book without pages—nice to see but lacking in substance.
- seek forgiveness and be humbled by their mortality.
- determine how adversity has enriched their meaning and purpose in life.
- journey inward and discover connections previously not understood or acknowledged.
- create an awareness of how the past interfaces with the present, and how the present ebbs back into the past.
- discover that the route to healing lies not only in the physical realm, but also in the emotional and spiritual realms.
- realize that the true significance of each unique story is that they can capture the spirit, the soul, and the genuine worth of the person who has died.
- come to understand that in their pain and suffering lies the awareness of the preciousness of each day on the earth.
- discover their truth in this present moment of time and space.

I believe that mourners can instinctively sense who can listen to their stories and who cannot. They often look for signs of open-heartedness and will gladly tell their stories to those they sense have a receptive spirit.

> "There is no greater agony than bearing an untold story inside you."
> — MAYA ANGELOU

The capacity to attend to your own stories of loss allows you to open your heart and connect to other people's stories.

Sometimes grief companions ask me how to remain patient when mourners feel the need to tell their same stories over and over again, session after session. This does happen, and when it does, it simply means that the mourner needs to keep telling the story to move from purely cognitive understanding to emotional-spiritual understanding. Keep in mind that this type of storytelling is not about conveying information. You and she both already know the information. It's about integrating the story into the very fabric of her being. So practice listening and being patient with this understanding in mind.

Honoring stories, both our own and others', requires that we slow down, turn inward, and create the sacred space to do so. Yes, this can be challenging in a fast-paced, efficiency-based culture in which many people lack an understanding of the value of telling the story. Yet companions realize that it is in having places to re-story their lives that mourners can embrace what needs to be embraced and come to understand that the human spirit prevails. We heal ourselves as we tell the tale. This is the awesome power of the story.

Leading

The skill of leading gives the mourner permission to tell you her story or expand on what has been said. As you know, people in grief will often have a need to explore events surrounding the death. This process is healing and is encouraged by the effective use of leading.

"The wise man doesn't give the right answers, he poses the right questions."

— CLAUDE LEVI-STRAUSS

There are two different kinds of leading—direct and indirect.

Direct leading is where you focus the area to be discussed more specifically. This allows the person to expand on some important area that has been brought into the discussion.

Examples:

"Could you tell me more about your husband's illness?

"You mentioned that the holidays are really difficult for you. Could you tell me more about that?"

Indirect leading often helps get the mourner started talking about whatever is important to him. It is general in nature and allows the person to explore his own ideas and sense of direction.

Examples:

"What else can you think of that might be helpful to talk about?"

"Do you have any lingering questions or thoughts?"

Pausing and looking expectantly at the other person can often serve as an indirect lead as well. This form of eye contact/body language lets the mourner know that you are ready to hear more about what she was just saying.

THE PHONE CALL FROM THE WELL-MEANING FAMILY MEMBER OR FRIEND

One day a concerned mother whose daughter had experienced a stillbirth called me and said, "It's been six months and she's still not 'over it.'"

Sometimes your caregiving will involve helping these family members and friends dispel misconceptions about grief. They often want the mourner back to the "old normal," and the faster, the better. Of course, this expectation is often anchored in our short social norms and grief-avoidant culture. Have grace as you offer support and understanding to people who have internalized such misconceptions.

In this particular case, after listening for a while you might do a bit of supportive confrontation and say, "It sounds like you care very much about your daughter. Would it be OK if we talked about how grief often progresses?" Then you can offer a bit of grief education, all the while affirming the caller's compassion and desire to help. Providing such insight and companioning tips over the phone will help others in the mourner's life help her.

Questioning

Questioning is one of the most important helping skills for companions. In addition to the practical utility of questions that help you understand the basics of the mourner's life and loss, your questions indicate your interest in listening and learning. Your questions also encourage the mourner to become more trusting and open with you and further explore areas he may have touched on only briefly. Ultimately, skillful questioning allows for more authentic mourning as well as deeper insight.

Open-ended questions

Open-ended questions are questions that cannot be answered with a yes or a no, a this or a that, but instead require a more developed explanation in response. Open-ended questions encourage self-exploration and are intentionally broad in nature. There is no right or wrong answer.

> *"I never learn anything talking. I only learn things when I ask questions."*
> — LOU HOLTZ

Most of the time, leading or open-ended questions are better questions for the grief companion to ask than closed or pointed questions. Open-ended questions give mourners the freedom to answer freely and self-determine the amount and kinds of information to share.

Examples:

"Could you tell me more about that?"

"How does that make you feel?"

"What would you like to talk about?"

"What is weighing on you most right now?"

or simply:

"I'm ready to listen." Or "I'm listening."

Closed-ended questions

Closed questions usually focus on factual content. They are

typically used to gather specific information and can be answered with a single word or a brief phrase.

In the counseling relationship, the use of too many closed questions can shut down the conversation. They are essentially dead ends and can make it feel like the companion is in charge of the conversation, not the mourner. A pattern of closed question followed by simple answer tells the mourner that you are the authority and that you know what is important to ask and talk about.

The mourner should never feel interrogated or subordinate to the companion. Instead, he should feel nurtured, important, and encouraged to talk openly and freely about whatever is on his mind and in his heart that day.

This is not to say that closed questions never have a place. You may sometimes want or need to ask simple follow-up questions as you work to understand the mourner's reality. For example, "How many years were you together?" or "Have you been sleeping well?" Try keeping closed questions to a minimum, however.

Here are some examples of closed-ended questions that you might choose to rephrase as open-ended questions instead:

CLOSED-ENDED:
How long was your dad sick?

OPEN-ENDED:
Could you tell me a little bit about your dad's illness?

CLOSED-ENDED:
Do you remember some good times?

OPEN-ENDED:
What are some of the times you remember best?

CLOSED-ENDED:

What do you miss most about your daughter?

OPEN-ENDED:

It sounds like your daughter was special to you in many ways. Can you tell me more about that?

CLOSED-ENDED:

Are you angry at your husband?

OPEN-ENDED:

I'm hearing some feelings of anger (or frustration or disappointment, etc.). Would you talk some more about that?

Questioning behavior

When you are asking questions, be sure to adjust your pace to that of the mourner. Going too slowly can suggest a lack of interest or understanding, while going too quickly implies impatience. Besides, if you ask rapid-fire questions without allowing the answers the mourner is giving you to hang and mellow for a bit, you may miss important but subtle opportunities to explore nuances.

Also, take care to never push anyone to reveal more than he is ready to reveal at the moment. Usually the trust relationship between grief companion and mourner must grow and develop before the deepest inner truths can be shared. What's more, part of the work of mourning involves dwelling in uncertainty and confusion for a time. Insight is often slow in coming, so it's not unusual for mourners to simply not yet *know* the answers to questions you might on the surface assume are simple or obvious.

Some questioning reminders:

• Evaluate the need to ask questions.

• When you ask a question, be aware that you are doing so.

- Carefully weigh the content and word choice of the questions you do ask.

- Examine the different kinds of questions available to you.

- Become sensitive to the questions the mourner asks of you, whether directly or indirectly.

INSTILLING HOPE

Grief companions instill and nurture hope in the mourners they care for. It is in having hope that you communicate your belief that the mourner can and will heal, or "become whole again."

Hope is an expectation of a good that is yet to be. It is an expression of the present alive with a sense of the possible. As a grief companion, you essentially lend your hope to the mourner by having hope in your heart and providing acceptance, recognition, affirmation, and gratitude in the context of your helping relationship. In dark, hopeless moments, he will be able to borrow your hope. Hope rallies energies and activates the courage to commit to mourning.

While the quality of hopefulness in a grief companion is about as easy to pin down as Jell-O, we all know it when we experience it in someone else. If you are genuinely, deep-down hopeful, you will not be able to help but communicate your hopefulness to mourners through all of your helping skills. Your body language will be hopeful. Your tone will be hopeful. Your paraphrasing and perception checking and summarizing will be hopeful.

"What oxygen is to the lungs, such is hope to the meaning of life."

— EMIL BRUNNER

This is definitely not to say that you should act overly cheerful or gloss over pain. No, you are never there to "buck her up." You must be willing and able to be present to profound pain, sometimes for long stretches of time, and believe in the necessity of sitting in the wound of grief. Yet, even as you are joining the mourner in her pain, you are present to her with the deep knowing that the pain is creating movement toward meaning and purpose. You use your companioning skills to help her, over time, fully explore and express her pain because you wholeheartedly believe in the transformative power of grief work.

Instilling and nurturing hope in the mourner even as you are present with him in the hurt is indeed an art. Finding ways to develop your own hopefulness outside your counseling office and fan the flames of hope before each companioning session will help you be the hope-filled grief companion you need to be.

Reflecting Feelings

Reflecting feelings is when you restate in fresh words the essential feelings, overtly stated or strongly implied, that the mourner has just expressed. This skill communicates an understanding of what the mourner is feeling and in essence says, "I am hearing you. I am with you." It can also help clarify vaguely expressed thoughts and feelings.

"Thoughts are the shadows of our feelings—always darker, emptier, and simpler."

— FRIEDRICH NIETZSCHE

Reflecting feelings is a close cousin of both paraphrasing and clarifying, but focuses on the underlying feelings being expressed more than the story or the factual details. The skill helps identify and name the feelings that the mourner is expressing.

Working as a professional or lay grief companion means working with people who are experiencing a wide range of feelings. In fact, feelings often dominate thoughts in acute grief. When mourners say they are "overwhelmed with grief," they usually mean they find themselves awash in strong and changing feelings that they cannot escape from. Being sensitive to those feelings, no matter what they are, is essential to successfully helping people in grief.

You will find that grieving people will come to you with a wide range of emotions. One person may openly express explosive emotions (such as anger), confusion, or relief, while another may be unexpressive, numb, or in total shock. What's more, some people wear their hearts on their sleeves, while others may have been culturally conditioned (by their culture or family of origin) to keep their true and most profound feelings hidden inside. The latter group will often need more time and trust-building as well as encouragement and gains in self-understanding to begin to acknowledge and express their true feelings.

As you work to understand and reflect back the mourner's feelings, keep these guidelines in mind:

• Feelings are never good or bad, they simply *are*.

• Everyone has a right to his or her unique feelings.

• Feelings always make sense when they are considered in the context of the person's individual life experience and worldview.

• Feelings are not dangerous (only actions can be dangerous).

• Denying or judging a feeling will not make it soften or go away. Only expression of the feeling can do that.

Remember that your job is *never* to minimize or take the mourner's feelings away. Instead, it is to compassionately bear witness to them and honor them. Especially for beginner grief companions, it is often tempting to "correct" or soothe away feelings that can be seen as harmful or inaccurate perceptions.

For example, it is common for mourners to feel guilty about a death for which they had no direct responsibility. Parents may feel guilty when a child dies, reasoning that they did something wrong or could/should have prevented it somehow. Spouses may share "if onlys" that speak of their regrets. As an empathetic helper, your instinct may be to reassure these mourners that there is no reason to feel regret, that they did nothing wrong. Yet what they need is not your assurance but your capacity to be present to them as they fully explore and feel and think through their natural and necessary regret.

Here are some examples of reflecting feelings statements (I've bolded the emotion that the grief companion names in the reflecting statement):

MOURNER:
"The words that the pastor used during the service held so much meaning for me."

GRIEF COMPANION:
"When you think about the message the pastor gave, you feel **comforted**."

MOURNER:
"She had been so sick for so long. It was hard on everyone. I'm glad she's no longer in pain."

GRIEF COMPANION:
"It sounds as if you are feeling **relieved** that she doesn't have to go through that anymore."

MOURNER:
"It's just so irresponsible of him to have left us like this! I find myself wanting to yell at him and tell him that what he did was not OK!"

GRIEF COMPANION:
"You sound **hurt** and **angry** about what he chose to do."

MOURNER:

"I don't even want to get out of bed in the morning. I don't want to do anything or go anywhere. Why should I? What does it matter?"

GRIEF COMPANION:

"It sounds like you are struggling with feelings of **hopelessness.**"

USING YOUR HELPING SKILLS OVER THE PHONE

Sometimes mourners literally call for help. Someone they love has been injured, is dying, or has recently died. They are in crisis and call 911, a funeral home, a hospice, a hospital, a hotline, or the organization you work with.

If you are on the receiving end of that phone call, how can you make use of your helping skills to effectively communicate compassion and support? You will not be doing long-term companioning with the caller, but you can still be a critical helper in that moment.

First, be an active listener. Listen carefully and fully. You will not have the additional feedback of the caller's body language and eye contact to rely upon, so you will have to focus all of your attention on the caller's words and tone of voice. Refrain completely from multitasking. Unless your task requires it, don't type or search on the computer or fill out paperwork while you listen.

Second, normalize and affirm. Mourners in crisis often feel like they are going crazy and project that they are handling the situation badly. Let them know that they are reacting normally to what is an abnormally intense situation. Use words of encouragement such as, "You're doing what you need to do right now," "I understand that this is hard," and "It's normal to feel _____ (afraid, scattered, or whatever the caller is communicating)."

Third, use your paraphrasing, clarifying, and other helping skills to make sure you understand what the mourner is communicating and to elicit additional information when it is needed. You will likely find that you need to do more leading over the phone—especially in crisis situations—than you would in person.

Fourth, match the tone and pace of the person who is speaking. This mirroring will help the caller feel understood and empathized with.

Fifth, speak clearly and repeat yourself when asked without frustration. People in acute grief have a naturally difficult time staying focused and have problems with short-term memory.

Sixth, be polite. Say please and thank you. Keep in mind that effective support is gentle and tentative.

Seventh, provide anticipatory guidance. Let the caller know what the next steps are and how and when they will happen.

Mourners in crisis often remember the compassionate support—or lack thereof—they receive over the phone. It's that important to them. Never underestimate the power of effective phone companioning skills.

Confronting

While the art of grief companioning is mostly about active, deep listening, affirming, and normalizing, occasionally it requires holding up the mirror of self-awareness for the mourner. You may sometimes need to confront mourners in order to bring them face-to-face with their own reality in cases when you witness an unbudging untruth or recalcitrant misperception that is blocking their movement toward hope and healing.

The word "confront" carries negative connotations, but keep in mind that supportive confrontation can be used to bring the mourner into more direct contact with her own experience, which can be the catalyst for change and movement to occur. Confrontation is difficult for most people because they have not experienced the use of this skill in a positive, growth-producing manner. As a matter of fact, many people come from families of origin in which confrontation was modeled as lecturing, judging, or acting in some punitive manner.

Because confrontation can be misused, it requires important self-exploration on the part of the grief companion before it is integrated into your counseling skills toolkit. Confronting means doing just what the word implies and not going beyond it. Confronting includes a description of the mourner's stated thoughts, feelings, beliefs, and/or behaviors. It should not contain an accusation, evaluation, or solution to the problem.

> *"I have sometimes made a poor choice by avoiding a necessary confrontation."*
> — JOHN CLEESE

Also, note that honest, supportive confrontation should come only after a helping alliance grounded in trust, warmth, and caring has already been well established. Confrontation should come from the heart, not just the head, and should only be used for behaviors that the mourner can control. Timing and pacing of confrontation is critical. If in doubt, wait.

Confrontation statements often focus on a "you said/but look" condition. The "you said" portion repeats or paraphrases something the mourner said, while the "but look" portion presents a contradiction or discrepancy. Here are some examples of appropriate, supportive confronting:

YOU SAID...
"I hear you say you have no support...

BUT LOOK...
Yet you have given me a number of examples of how people in your life are supporting you."

YOU SAID...

"You acknowledge the need to mourn your mother's death...

BUT LOOK...

Yet you seem to keep avoiding looking too closely at the relationship you had with her."

YOU SAID...

"You've told me you want a better relationship with your husband...

BUT LOOK...

But I have also perceived that you don't tend to communicate openly with him, especially about your grief."

YOU SAID...

"You emphasize how close you were to your sister...

BUT LOOK...

But you have also said that you rarely saw her in recent years."

When used well, your confronting skills will not shame the mourner or make him feel inferior but instead help him understand a truth that his unawareness of was holding him hostage or keeping him stuck.

Effective confronting creates clearer self-perception for the mourner, allows for new self-exploration, creates opportunities for both insight and behavior change, results in deeper trust between the companion and the mourner, and encourages growth and self-actualization.

Summarizing

Summarizing is a method of tying together several ideas and feelings at the end of a period of discussion or a counseling session. It helps the mourner realize that you have really focused in on what she has said. It is an excellent way to check on the accuracy of what has been shared and understood, clearing up any confusion that may have arisen. In addition, summarizing is a natural way to make transitions from one content area to another, or to simply conclude an interaction.

> "It is an absolute human certainty that no one can know his own beauty or perceive a sense of his own worth until it has been reflected back to him in the mirror of another loving, caring human being."
>
> — JOHN JOSEPH POWELL

During stressful times, people usually want a clear understanding of their situation and what decisions they have made. Refining your use of the skill of summarizing will help you better accomplish this sense of increased understanding and awareness. As you probably realize, when someone else summarizes decisions you have made or concerns you have, it often gives you a heightened, clearer understanding of the situation. It also lends a feeling of movement, direction, and purpose to the session and toward the next session to come.

Here are some natural ways to lead into your summary:

- "Before we end our time together today, maybe it would be helpful to review what we have talked about…"

- "I'd like to take a minute to go over what you have explored today…"

- "Thank you for sharing with me today. I heard you say…"

Sometimes summarizing can also be used to begin a session:

- "Last time we talked about how you loved your mom, but you didn't always like her."

REFINING YOUR HELPING SKILLS

You can't be an effective grief companion if your basic counseling skills are not effective. The good news is that they can be learned, practiced, and enhanced.

As you begin to learn or refine these skills, you will probably find yourself concentrating more than ever before on communication behaviors whenever you have a conversation (or even observe others interacting). This is certainly natural and may result in some initial feelings of discomfort and tension. With time, however, you will find yourself relaxing and discovering that the learning process is very rewarding.

You will probably find yourself proceeding through four distinct phases as you work on your counseling skills:

PHASE 1: **Initial learning**
You may feel excited about learning new things and afraid that you're not a "natural" at it. Just remember that with appropriate training and practice, you can become an effective communicator!

PHASE 2: **Uncomfortable use**
In this phase you're learning how to use your new skills, but you may feel mechanical and even "fake." You don't feel spontaneous because you have to think carefully as you attempt to use any new skill.

PHASE 3: **Consciously skilled**
In this phase you begin to use the skills more effectively. However, you continue to be self-conscious. You are getting better, but the skills may still feel somewhat mechanical. You do begin to use language that is natural for you.

PHASE 4: **Naturally skilled**

This final phase occurs only after you have worked through the training and practiced the skills extensively. You must use the skills on a daily basis over an extended time to get to this level of skill. When you achieve this level, the skills come naturally and comfortably without you even consciously thinking about them.

If you are an experienced grief companion, you may well already be good at the helping skills. However, I find that even longtime companions—me included—typically can be helped by a skills refresher. All professionals have their strengths and weaknesses, and over time those strengths and weaknesses tend to wear deep grooves. We're good at what we're good at, but we don't often work to identify, acknowledge, and get better at what we're not so good at. Which of the helping skills in this section are you not so good at? I challenge you to identify and work on those.

Also remember that as you progress through these four phases of learning, you will regress from time to time. Don't give up! This regression is a normal part of any new learning experience. Keep envisioning yourself comfortably interacting with grieving people at Phase 4—and you will get there. As you learn, relax and don't berate yourself when you don't immediately use each skill to the best of your ultimate capability.

Practice, practice, practice!

INTERFACING THE HELPING SKILLS AND THE SIX NEEDS OF MOURNING

As a grief companion, you will walk alongside the mourner on the journey through grief. You will rely on mourner-centered talk therapy (or just plain attentive listening) as the bedrock on the path. As you walk and talk, you will also be on the watch for the six trail markers or needs of mourning that we reviewed on pages 41 through 47.

Every time the mourner naturally moves toward one of the mourning needs (and she will, because they are innate), it is your companioning skills you will use to make the most of the opportunity. Through genuine empathy and a skillful mix of attending, nonverbal communication, paraphrasing, perception checking, clarifying, and the other skills in your interpersonal toolkit, you will help the mourner meet a bit more of his normal and necessary mourning need while simultaneously gracing him with the feeling of cathartic progress the encounter unlocks.

"The real heroes anyway aren't the people doing things; the real heroes are the people NOTICING things, paying attention."

— JOHN GREEN

I'm not saying you should cry out, "Hey look! You're working on defining your new self-identity! That's mourning need 4!" (Definitely don't do that. ☺) Rather, I'm suggesting that you silently notice the encounter with the mourning need and use your companioning skills to help the grieving person in your care explore the territory to the limits of his energy and desire on that day. Skillful paraphrasing, clarifying, and summarizing, for example, may enable him to glimpse and feel his own progress.

As you use your helping skills to facilitate the mourner's encounters with the six needs of mourning, you must also be on the watch for her unique strengths and ways of being. Those strengths can help her meet her needs of mourning, and when you call attention to them and help her see them, you are appropriately revealing her to herself in ways that can synergize her journey to healing.

Grief companions have the privilege of helping the grieving people in their care experience what I call "divine momentum." Divine momentum is the notion that the process of mourning naturally and necessarily leads to healing and reconciliation. In other words, every time they meet (or re-meet) a need of mourning, mourners move forward. They experience "perturbation"—the movement that enables change. To trust in divine momentum is to believe that healing can and will unfold.

> "It's not enough to have lived. We should be determined to live for something. May I suggest that it be creating joy for others, sharing what we have for the betterment of person-kind, bringing hope to the lost and love to the lonely."
>
> — LEO BUSCAGLIA

As a grief companion, you unleash and continue to nurture divine momentum by using your self as instrument and by making use of your helping skills to facilitate effective encounters with the six needs of mourning. I encourage you to memorize the six needs of mourning. If and when appropriate, I also encourage you to help the mourner learn about the six needs of mourning. Then, as you walk alongside her on the journey through grief, you will both be better prepared to embrace them as they naturally arise.

PART THREE:

THE SUMMIT

AND NOW WE COME TO THE END SECTION OF THIS
BOOK AS WELL AS THE FINAL PHASE OF THE MOURNER'S
JOURNEY.

Many grief-care models refer to the goal of therapy as "resolution"
or "recovery."

*"Stand tall on the
summit after a
tedious climb. Take
in the remarkable
scenery and the
exhilaration of
accomplishment."*

— RICHELLE E. GOODRICH

Yet in my personal as well as professional
experience, we are all changed by the
experience of loss and grief. The notion
of recovery, as it is understood by many,
implies an absolute, a perfect state of re-
establishment.

"Reconciliation" is a term I believe more
accurately describes what unfolds as the
mourner works to integrate the new
reality of moving forward in life without
the physical presence of the person who died. Even when we have
fully and actively mourned, we as human beings never "get over"
our grief but instead become reconciled to it. It becomes a part
of who we are. What's more, "griefbursts"—sudden moments of
intense pain—will continue forever.

Like grief itself, reconciliation is a process, not a moment in time or a discrete "finish line." Working through the emotional relationship with the person who died and re-directing energy and initiative toward the future often take longer and involve more effort than most people are aware.

> "Grief can be the garden of compassion. If you keep your heart open through everything, your pain can become your greatest ally in your life's search for love and wisdom."
>
> — RUMI

When mourners begin to approach the summit of reconciliation, they find a renewed sense of energy and confidence, an ability to fully acknowledge the reality of the death, and the capacity to become re-involved with the activities of living. They also are able to acknowledge that pain and grief are difficult yet necessary parts of life and living.

Reconciliation is the stage of the journey in which the full reality of the death becomes a part of the mourner. Beyond an intellectual working through is an emotional and spiritual embracing. What had been understood at the "head" level is now understood at the "heart" level—someone loved is dead. When a reminder such as holidays, anniversaries, or other special memories are triggered, the mourner still experiences the pain of grief, yet the duration and intensity of the pain is typically less severe as healing continues.

In reconciliation, the ever-present, sharp, and stinging pain of grief dulls to an acknowledged feeling of loss that has given rise to renewed meaning and purpose. The sense of loss does not completely disappear yet softens, and the intense pangs of grief become less frequent. Hope for a continued life emerges as the griever is able to make commitments to the future, realizing that the dead person will never be forgotten, yet knowing that one's own life can and will move forward.

On the way to the summit, the effective grief companion fosters the hope of reconciliation. The majority of mourners experience a loss of confidence and self-esteem that leaves them questioning their capacity to heal. Grief companions who project a willingness to hope and anticipate reconciliation assist mourners in movement toward their grief instead of away from it.

SIGNS OF RECONCILIATION IN GRIEF

Not every person will exhibit all of these signs. However, most of them should be present for the mourner to be considered in the final and forever phase of her grief journey.

- A recognition of the reality and finality of the death (in both the head and heart).
- A return to stable eating and sleeping patterns that were present prior to the death.
- A renewed sense of energy and personal well-being.
- A subjective sense of release or relief from the person who has died (they have thoughts of the person, but are not preoccupied with these thoughts).
- The capacity to enjoy experiences in life that should normally be enjoyable.
- The establishment of new and healthy relationships.
- The capacity to live a full life without feelings of guilt or lack of self-respect.
- The capacity to organize and plan one's life toward the future.
- The capacity to become comfortable with the way things are rather than attempting to make things as they were.

- The capacity to being open to more change in one's life.

- The awareness that one has allowed oneself to fully mourn and has survived. The awareness that one does not "get over grief," but instead is able to acknowledge, "This is my new reality and I am ultimately the one who must work to create new meaning and purpose in my life."

- The capacity to acknowledge new parts of one's self that have been discovered in the growth through one's grief.

- The capacity to adjust to the new role changes that have resulted from the loss of the relationship.

- The capacity to be compassionate with oneself when normal resurgences of intense grief occur (holidays, anniversaries, special occasions).

- The capacity to acknowledge that the pain of loss is an intrinsic part of life that results from the ability to give and receive love.

I have found that many grieving people try to convince themselves and others that they are further along in the healing process than they really are. They have possibly made some progress on the path, but with your experience and wisdom you can see that they are actually far from exhibiting most or all of the signs of reconciliation.

It's kind of like hiking a long, unfamiliar trail in the Rocky Mountains near my home. I may hike and climb, huff and puff, stopping now and then to say, "Surely I'm almost there..."—only to find out after I've continued on for several more hours and that what I assumed all those miles ago was the final ascent was in fact only another bump in the road.

In grief (as in most things), only hindsight is 20/20. As companion, you can support the laboring mourner on the arduous path to healing by remembering the mantra: "No rewards for speed, not attached to outcome, divine momentum."

Even as we grief companions expect the grief journey to be long and painful, when we expect reconciliation, and know it is possible, we help the mourner hold reconciliation as a realistic hope. However, if we as helpers somehow collaborate with those mourners who perceive that they will never move beyond the acute pain of their grief, we may well become a hindrance to their eventual healing.

Reconciliation from grief is normal. Yet people need support, compassion, patience, perseverance, determination, and, perhaps most of all, hope and the belief in their capacity to heal. Part of the helping role is to nurture conditions outside the person and qualities within the person that make healing possible.

As you work to support the reconciliation process, you do not impose your own direction on the content of what is explored; rather, you allow the direction of the mourner's experience to guide what you do and to help determine how you respond in supportive, life-enhancing ways. You appreciate the person as being independent from you and respect his right to determine the direction of the companioning relationship.

The process of helping another human being restore and renew herself calls upon all of your personal strengths and helping skills. The mourner will work hard, and so will you. But the summit of reconciliation makes the journey worthwhile. It is such a special—if bittersweet—place, with views that seem to stretch on forever. Only at the summit can the mourner can look back and fully see how treacherous was the path to get there. Only at the summit can the mourner turn in all directions and look out on his past as well as his future, which includes more unknown paths and summits.

Whenever you help a mourner reach the summit of reconciliation, take a moment to celebrate and have gratitude. I believe there is no more important work in life. Companioning our fellow human beings through many dark days in the tangled wilderness of despair is indeed challenging, but the rewards of reaching reconciliation are glorious for both the mourner and you. Just think—without you and your commitment, empathy, compassion, and skilled helping, many grievers would never emerge from the darkness. They would stay forever lost. They would die while they were still alive. But instead, you made it possible for them to save themselves.

> *"Peace is a journey of a thousand miles, and it must be taken one step at a time."*
> — LYNDON B. JOHNSON

ON BEING UNATTACHED TO OUTCOME

Effective grief companions are not attached to outcome. That is, they are present to whatever the mourner is expressing in the moment and not focusing on how and when the mourner will emerge from the wilderness. Yet at the same time, the companion is exuding hope and faith that the emergence— reconciliation—will come.

> *"Compassion stands on the pillars of trust, love, awareness, and detachment."*
> — AMIT RAY

Is this an oxymoron? Is it possible to remain detached from outcome while at the same time walking alongside the mourner with an intentional focus on the six needs of mourning and an understanding of and hope for reconciliation?

Yes, it is possible! Staying unattached to outcome involves remaining alongside, not leading, and also being open to whatever comes next.

Mourners will surprise you. Their paths are rarely predictable, even to those of us who have borne witness to many grief journeys. If you remain in the moment with the mourner while trusting that through active mourning and effective companioning she will eventually reach her unique version of reconciliation, you are remaining unattached to outcome.

As the Zen statement observes in a lovely way, "Spring comes, and the grass grows all by itself." The grief companion both marvels at this growth and expects it.

SELF-CARE FOR THE GRIEF COMPANION

You may have heard the Cherokee legend about the two wolves. In an effort to pass along his hard-won wisdom, a tribal elder tells his grandson about the battle that rages inside him.

"Two wolves are fighting inside me," he says. "One is evil—full of anger, envy, arrogance, self-pity, ego, and resentment. The other is good—full of love, hope, generosity, serenity, humility, empathy, and compassion. The same wolves are battling inside you and everyone else."

"Which wolf will win?" asks the wide-eyed child.

The elder replies, "The one you feed."

"Growing into your future with health and grace and beauty doesn't have to take all your time. It rather requires a dedication to caring for yourself as if you were rare and precious, which you are, and regarding all life around you as equally so, which it is."
— VICTORIA MORAN

As a grief companion, your self-care commitment and habits (or lack thereof) are what feed your wolves. Notice that the good wolf represents not only the ways of being that will make your own life happier and more meaningful, but they are also the helping qualities and skills you need to be an effective grief companion.

"For those of you who struggle with guilt regarding self-care, answer this question: What greater gift can you give to those you love than your own wholeness?"

— SHANNON TANNER

In other words, good self-care activates and reinforces your helping skills.

We've talked a lot about the concept of "companioning" our fellow human beings in grief in this book. Now I want you to turn the companioning lens on yourself. Can one companion oneself in life and in caregiving?

Yes! Self-companionship is a journey of uncovering, connecting with, and nurturing your own soul. To companion yourself is to look with compassion at your own soul and to nurture the divine spark you find there.

Self-companionship for grief companions involves exploring and mourning your own griefs, discovering your own mythologies about helping others, being watchful for signs of burnout, acknowledging any work-life imbalances you may have, revealing your vision for rebalancing your life, scheduling self-care and spirit time into every day, carving out more sacred downtime weekly, monthly, and yearly, and actively seeking joy.

While the details of how to go about each of these self-companioning steps is outside the scope of this resource, I do encourage you to read my book *Companioning You! A Soulful Guide to Caring for Yourself While You Care for the Dying and the*

Bereaved. After all, feeding the right wolf is as essential to your companioning effectiveness as the counseling skills are that we covered in Part Two. I would also argue that unless you are good at empathizing with, listening to, and being present to your own self, you can't really be effective at those ways of being with others.

So feed the good wolf. Please. You deserve it—and so do the mourners in your care.

BEGINNING AGAIN WITH EACH NEW MOURNER

The more you companion mourners, the more you will practice your helping skills and the more comfortable and skillful you will become at using them. You will reach Phase 4 of companioning we talked about on page 90. Then what?

> "*The most common ego identifications have to do with possessions, the work you do, social status and recognition, knowledge and education... None of these is you.*"
>
> — ECKHART TOLLE

First, I strongly believe that we are never done learning. There is always more to learn about ourselves as well as about the mysterious journey we call grief and the companioning philosophy and helping skills. Read books. Take classes. Engage regularly with other grief companions to learn from one another.

Second, continue to work on your own self-care, because your self-as-instrument also needs lavish attention.

And third, learn to come to each new companioning relationship with a beginner's mind and heart. Part of creating divine momentum for the mourner is to honor his unique story as if it is the first time you ever heard it—because it is. While the experienced companion will have borne witness to many similar stories, for each unique mourner you are unearthing a treasure trove of particulars—the nature of the relationship, the circumstances of the death, the mourner's loss history, spiritual beliefs, etc. Your active empathy will drive your compassionate curiosity, and you will genuinely feel humbled in the process of supporting the mourner.

While you may one day find yourself in the "zone" of grief companioning—effectively walking alongside mourners and helping them do their work of mourning without having to consciously think about what you are saying or doing—you will still and always need to find ways to assume the role of the novice or learner in each new relationship. You must meet each new mourner with humility.

For the experienced grief companion, this can be a challenging conundrum. You have gained skills and even expertise, yet you can never be the expert. You know so much, yet you must join the new mourner at the trailhead assuming nothing. The ego likes to be fawned over and held on a pedestal. One thing that helps me maintain my beginner's mind and heart is the "ritual of reception" I take time for before every counseling session. (See page 111.) I also long ago relinquished any hubris our hierarchical culture encouraged me to carry for the Ph.D. that goes after my name. It only means I did my best to learn about the mysterious body of grief knowledge There's only one way for me to learn about you and your grief, and that is by raptly listening to you.

QUESTIONS AND ANSWERS

As a veteran grief counselor and educator, I'm often asked questions by beginning grief companions about a variety of theoretical and practical topics. They want to know how I handle certain recurring situations or issues. Here are the questions I'm most frequently asked and the answers I give.

Q. You write and teach about the need to "feel grief to heal grief." But aren't there some people who don't need to feel as much as others?

A.   I do often speak of how feeling love requires humans to feel the counterpoint to that love, which is grief. I do believe this. However, some people have misinterpreted this to mean that I believe that everyone must feel deeply and emote strongly.

Not so. It is vital for grief companions to be respectful of each mourner's unique emotionality and grieving style. Some people have never been demonstrative with their feelings, particularly those of affection and loss. These people will naturally be more reserved in their mourning. At the same time, however, it's important for the grief companion to help reserved mourners feel safe enough to express feelings that they might normally hide. In other words, just because they are not usually expressive does not mean they aren't feeling deeply. And if they are feeling deeply, they need tools for the expression of those feelings. If mourner-led talk therapy all by itself isn't the tool for the job, you might encourage these mourners to try other methods, such as journaling and music therapy (music being an amazing tool for helping people access emotionality).

And then there is the subgroup of mourners who seem to

neither feel deeply nor emote strongly. In the companioning relationship, a mourner's lack of deep grief feelings may simply mean that he never formed a strong attachment to the person who died, in which case it would be normal for him to not need to grieve and mourn deeply. More typically in my companioning experience, however, reserved mourners do feel deeply inside and are coming to you for help in connecting with and expressing their emotional selves.

Doka and Martin (2010) have contributed a valuable overview of different grieving styles on a continuum, with what they define as intuitive grievers on one end of the spectrum (people who "tend to express feelings and wish to talk about their experience with others") and what they call instrumental grievers on the other end of the spectrum (people who "tend to grieve more cognitively and tend to express their grief in terms of thoughts, analysis, and actions").

I once counseled a very intellectual, retired university professor, who came to me after his wife's death. He was definitely an instrumental griever. I went very slowly with him and kept looking for ways to help him access his emotions. His wife had been a poet, and at my suggestion, he eagerly took on the task of collecting her work together. He brought the collection to our sessions, and we began the ritual of ending each session with him reading aloud one of her poems, chosen at random in that moment. He found this addition to our sessions meaningful. Her poems seemed to bypass his brain and directly touch his tender heart. As he read, he cried. And as he cried, he slowly, week by week, began to integrate her death into his continuing life. Had we not found a way for him to access his profound emotions—which were there all along, of course—he would not have been able to reconcile his grief as well as he did.

Yes, we as grief companions must join mourners where they are before we can help them move themselves, slowly and in doses. Love is the emotion that forms every attachment, and where there is love and loss, there is not only intellectual or cognitive grief but also emotional grief. It will vary in amplitude, and every mourner will come to you with a different natural style of expressing it, but rest assured, it's there (except in cases of lack of attachment).

Q. **Sometimes I find myself getting emotional along with the mourner. What are your thoughts on that?**

A. This is one of the most frequent questions I get from my training workshop participants. Many grief companions—new and experienced alike—think that any expression of sadness, such as crying, by the caregiver is unprofessional and should never happen. I disagree. I often say: If you do this work and never cry—worry. However, if you cry all the time—see a therapist.

Actually, the answer is that it can sometimes be a good thing and sometimes be a bad thing. You are human. You are using your self as instrument. You are practicing empathy. When you open your heart to mourners, of course their losses will touch your heart. I certainly hope you will be touched. However, if you are constantly feeling overly emotional and tearing up during sessions—in other words, if you can't make it through a session without crying or being as or more emotional than the mourner—you might need to attend to your own personal grief or life issues.

I once companioned a couple whose six-year-old child had recently been killed—accidentally run over by someone else in their driveway. They were so in shock and distress that they could hardly speak. To open my heart to them required me to join them where they were. At our first session especially, they were emotional. I was emotional. We were human beings responding to a traumatic, life-changing event. Our shared emotionality was not only normal and necessary, it helped us quickly bond. They trusted me because I made it clear I could understand their horror and pain.

I always encourage grief companions to have a responsibility partner—another caregiver with whom they can debrief and who has the wherewithal and wisdom to advise about caregiving matters.

Q. Are what you term "griefbursts" normal?

A.   Oh yes, quite normal. Griefbursts (which some authors refer to as "grief attacks") are sudden and often powerful bursts of emotion that seem to come out of nowhere. They typically take mourners by surprise. They may be going about their day, not thinking about the death at that moment, when something as simple as a smell, a sound, or a place brings the full force of their loss down upon them. Their grief "bursts" in on them.

Because grief never discretely ends, griefbursts are great reminders that love never dies. While authentic mourning softens grief over time, grief will recapture our attention throughout our lifetimes. In addition to random sensory details, triggers include nodal events such as the anniversary of the death, birthdays, graduations, weddings, births of babies, and other loss experiences.

Feel honored when the mourner chooses to recount a griefburst experience with you or even have one in your presence! Listen, learn, and support.

Q. What do I do about mourners who tell me their main coping tactic is to stay really busy?

A. The first thing to keep in mind is that denial and distraction are healthy coping mechanisms—especially soon after a loss. Mourners do what they need to do to survive. As grief companions, we should not immediately try to tear down their natural defenses. Next, consider the grief-avoidant culture in which we live. "Just keep busy" is one of the most common pieces of advice mourners receive. Also, some grievers were busy bees before their loss. They're just the kind of people who can't sit still, who have to be constantly doing and/or interacting. And finally, mourning must be done in doses. Even long after the loss, it's essential for mourners to encounter then evade, encounter then evade. If they tried to mourn full-time, they would die of a broken heart.

But even after all of this is taken into account, you will still find that some grievers are using busy-ness too much and for too long as a means of actively avoiding their grief. If a grief thought or feeling arises, rather than sitting with it, embracing it, and finding ways to express it, they will instead jump up and find something to do—something so distracting that it pushes the grief aside. What was a healthy coping mechanism at first has become a habit of avoidance.

When you see this happening, one way to counteract it is to project a calm unhurriedness. The busy bee types often have frenetic energy. In the presence of your "no rewards for speed" and "unattached to outcome" aura, they may also slow down. And with careful timing and pacing, you might need to reach into your counseling skills toolkit and pull out your confronting skill. Supportively and compassionately confronting a griever who remains stuck as a result of his self-distraction habit can be a gift. However, simply pointing out the avoidance is usually not enough. Such grievers often need tips and tools for embracing and expressing their grief. They tend to be task-oriented, and giving them emotional-spiritual tasks to try is helpful. My book *Healing Your Grieving Soul*, for example, contains a number of spiritual activities that provide structured encounters with grief.

Q. **Are there times when I should encourage grievers to mourn outside of their family systems?**

A. We have all probably heard the misconception that families get closer at a time of death. Actually, while this may be true initially after a death in the family, in the following weeks and months we often witness what I call the "pressure cooker" phenomenon. This is when everyone in the family impacted by the death has a high need to feel understood and little capacity to be understanding. In other words, when family members experience the same loss, they may not be able to support each other. This sets the family up for conflict and confrontation. When you sense that this is happening, you will need to help normalize this phenomenon and help the person you are companioning get support outside the family.

In addition, after a traumatic death or after a long period of caregiving, the family may be drained and depleted. They may lack the energy to deal with longstanding family dynamics.

There is often a ripple effect of issues that come to the surface after such a death.

If you want to enhance your body of knowledge in this area, you may want to consider some additional training in family counseling. Personally, I was trained as a family therapist and have found that to be invaluable in my work with grieving people.

Q. **I sometimes find myself wanting to share my own experiences with those I companion. What are your thoughts on that?**

A. You are referring to what in counseling training is called "self-disclosure"—sharing your own experiences at appropriate times in the helping process (the key word being "appropriate"). This area of helping skills has so much to do with timing and pacing.

For example, if you felt a need to start out every encounter with the mourner by sharing your own story, odds are that this is more about your need than it is about her need. I commonly see this in people who try to quickly place themselves in helping roles after their own loss experiences. If you were to find this happening, consider that you might need to spend more time in the receiving mode before you enter the giving mode.

Here are some rules of thumb about self-disclosure:

- Be aware of your timing and pacing.

- The focus should be more on the mourner than on you. Always ask yourself before sharing: How might this self-disclosure help the mourner?

- A good ratio to keep is mind is 80-20: You should be doing no more than 20 percent of the talking, including self-disclosure as well as all of the other verbal counseling skills we've reviewed in this book. The mourner should be doing at least 80 percent of the talking. If ever I find myself creeping above the 20 percent threshold, I know that I am at risk for trying to direct their grief or fix them.

Very early in my career, I was counseling a grieving little boy who announced in the middle of a session, "You're talking too much." I was new and nervous. I wanted to help him. But he was right. I was over-caretaking. Thanks to his vocal honesty, I quickly learned to rein in my instinct to talk too much.

• Some mourners will ask you very directly and early on in your relationship about your loss history because they believe this is essential to your ability to understand and support them. For other mourners, your loss history may not even come up. If they do ask, it's an appropriate time for self-disclosure. If they don't ask, don't tell.

• When companioning grieving teens, I never tell them up front that when I was their age, one of my best friends died of leukemia. Yet after a session or two, almost always they will ask me why I do what I do, and then I will share the story of my friend.

• If you are doing a great deal of self-disclosure with a mourner, ask yourself why. Is this more about your potential need to "re-story" your own life? If so, make use of your responsibility partner to reflect on what is going on for you.

Q. I've heard you encourage grief caregivers in your trainings to develop what you called a "readiness to receive" ritual. What is that about?

A. Over the years I have discovered the value of a spiritual practice I use to prepare my heart and soul to be present to mourners with humility, unknowing, and unconditional love. I have come to refer to this practice as my "readiness to receive" ritual.

Just before I see anyone for support in their journey, I center myself in a quiet place, inside or outside the Center for Loss and Life Transition. By creating a sacred space and stepping away from the business of the day, I seek to find quiet and stillness. In a very real sense, I'm preparing my soul to be totally present to the grieving person or family. This practice is a way of letting go of anything that might get in the way of my open-heartedness. I seem to need this time to listen to myself before I can listen to others.

Once I have gone quiet, I repeat a three-phrase mantra to myself:

"No rewards for speed."

"Not attached to outcome."

"Divine momentum."

These words help me slow down, recognize my role is to help create momentum for the griever to authentically mourn, and remember the vital importance of being present to people where they are instead of where I might think they need to be. After repeating these phrases for two to three minutes— almost in meditation—I usually conclude with some sort of affirmation like, "I thank the universe for providing me the opportunity to help people mourn well so they can go on to live well and love well."

I encourage you to try my ritual of reception or create your own. Anything that helps prepare you to be present to the mourner and embody the companioning philosophy will work.

Q. **What should I know about training, credentialing, and how I can refer to myself as a caregiver?**

A. This is important to know, of course, because you don't want to get yourself into trouble. Laws govern who can hang their shingle as a grief counselor or therapist. Requirements for level of education and degrees vary from state to state and province to province, and it is important to be aware of the requirements in the area in which you practice. Some states and provinces have licensure and a regulatory body that oversees counseling practices. (If you are a lay grief companion, you can call yourself a grief support person but not a counselor or therapist.)

Most people who provide formal grief counseling have advanced degrees in disciplines such as counseling, social work, or pastoral ministry. Beyond a general degree, many grief companions engage in further study in death education and counseling. In this context, they are able to learn skills more specific to the theory, research, and practice of grief care. You will find there is a spectrum of education/training experiences available ranging from one-day workshops to undergraduate and graduate degrees in thanatology.

An organization in this field to be aware of and strongly consider joining is the Association for Death Education and Counseling. They have a certification program that acknowledges people have demonstrated a foundational body of knowledge in the field of thanatology. You can review these certification requirements on their website at adec.org.

Our Center for Loss certification in "Death and Grief Studies" requires 150 hours of study of the body of knowledge as outlined in our training catalog. (Details at centerforloss.com.) The certification we provide in collaboration with Colorado State University does not require a specific educational background because we believe in the value of training people ranging from lay people to psychiatrists. We always remind our graduates that this certification is not an indication of clinical competence and that they need to abide by state or province requirements for any formal counseling practice.

Finally, a word of caution about using the term "grief companion" too freely. I know of a woman who has come to the Center for Loss, learned my model of grief care, and began to use it in her work in her community. She ended up in contact with a widower who wrongly assumed that grief "companion" meant something else entirely.

Q. **You refer to the need for mourners to have safe places or "sanctuaries" where they can mourn openly and honestly. How do you define sanctuary?**

A. A sanctuary is a place of refuge from external demands. It is a space in which the mourner is free to disengage from the outside world. A place where the need to turn inward and suspend will not be hurried or ridiculed. Your companioning space is the mourner's oasis—maybe the only place in which she can turn her full attention to her grief and think, feel, and express it fully without fear of judgment.

Q. **I've heard about something called the "new science of grief." What is it, and how does it compare to your philosophy of grief care?**

A. In other books, magazine articles, and websites, you may run across a philosophy (and even "studies") that purports that humans are resilient and do not need to express their grief or receive support for it. The "new science of grief," as it is sometimes called, essentially claims that people "get over" grief on their own, over time, and that grief naturally heals itself.

However, scientific findings cannot measure a soul-based experience that is not easily measured. As Albert Einstein astutely observed, "Not everything that is meaningful is measurable." Moreover, scientific research on grief may well reinforce our culture's desire to avoid grief instead of befriending it.

I find it interesting that the same medical establishment that is promoting "the new science of grief" simultaneously champions the medicalization of depression. How can we "get over" our grief on our own, without any expression or support, yet need therapy and often antidepressants for our depression? It's contradictory, oxymoronic thinking that (as you can tell) not only irks me but further harms the millions of people who are hurting and need help.

People do need to mourn their grief to heal it, and they do need and deserve the love and care of others along the way, including, at times, the lifeline of a grief support group and the companionship of a skilled grief counselor. To mourn is to find their way back to a life of joy and love.

Q. **How can I stay sensitive to each unique mourner's spiritual or religious orientation?**

A. In the mosaic world in which we live, you're right to work on finding ways to learn more about each mourner's religious and spiritual background. Some people say there's no God. Some people are very religious. And many others are in the middle somewhere. As one woman told me after the sudden accidental death of her daughter, "If there is a God, he is on a long spring break."

I use the following Spiritual Assessment checklist to help me keep track of what I'm learning about each mourner's spiritual/religious orientation. Please note that it's not to be filled out interview style! I do not sit the mourner down and begin bombarding him with all of these questions. Instead, as he naturally expresses spiritual beliefs or questions in our sessions, after the session I make a few notes on this worksheet. I might occasionally ask a clarifying or follow-up question that uncovers more of this information. Eventually I have a spiritual profile for the mourner that I can glance at for a quick summary or refresher.

For me, knowing all or most of the information in the checklist helps me walk alongside the mourner as he searches for meaning and affirm spiritual "aha!"s when they occur.

SPIRITUAL ASSESSMENT CHECKLIST
(Note that for all items on this list, I use the word "spiritual," but I also mean to include religious beliefs and experiences.)

- Spiritual background
- Place of worship/spiritual home

- Clergyperson or spiritual guide
- Friends or family members who provide spiritual support
- Beliefs about and relationship with God
- Ways in which spiritual beliefs and practices may have changed since the loss
- Current spiritual practices
- Spiritual symbols important to mourner
- Books or other resources that provide spiritual comfort
- Beliefs and questions about the afterlife
- Things mourner finds calms or feeds spirit
- Ideas for integrating spiritual care into the mourner's holistic care plan

Q. What are your thoughts about after-death communication?

A. Over my almost 40 years of supporting my fellow humans in grief, I have had numerous mourners report signs or visions of the person who died—sensing a presence, hearing a voice, feeling a touch, smelling a fragrance, visitation dreams, etc. These experiences usually bring comfort, reassurance, and hope to the mourner.

Such reports are so common that they should not be perceived as "pathological" or "crazy." I'm always honored when people feel safe enough with me to share them. Keep in mind that in many other part of the world, such experiences are openly talked about with no judgment. Sadly, in our North American culture, the mourner has to be selective in choosing a confidant.

I have also learned that it's critically important for me as a grief companion to know what I believe about the afterlife and after-death communication. In my sessions with mourners, it is my role to believe in their truth. In other words, I believe that they believe what they are telling me. But I must also be aware of my own beliefs because if I am not, it's harder for me to guard against the often subtle comments or even body language that hint at judgment. And for the record, what do I believe about the afterlife? I'm open to the mystery.

Q. **You recently invited people to join you in championing what you call the "Slow Grief" movement. Can you explain more about that?**

A. The Slow Grief movement acknowledges that loss is as much a part of the human experience as love. It recognizes that loss changes us forever and that grief is a normal, necessary, and, yes, sssllllooowwww process. It also proclaims the need for people to express their grief and to be supported by their communities. And it asks us to look to the past to recapture the healing wisdom and customs we have almost lost, such as meaningful funeral experiences instead of having parties.

In the Slow Food movement, many elementary schools are planting edible gardens to teach children where food comes from and what actual food looks and tastes like. In the Slow Grief movement, perhaps we can incorporate simple rituals and sacred spaces into elementary schools that help young children explore their natural instincts to be open and honest about all feelings, including the so-called dark emotions of loss.

In the same vein, in our efforts to rein in medical costs and champion the wellness model over the sickness model that has predominated for a number of decades now, we are re-examining when and how best to use, judiciously, prescription drugs, diagnostic procedures, and surgeries. In the Slow Grief movement, it's time to remove grief from the purview of medicine altogether. Let's strike it from the list of illnesses and take it back as a normal, natural, and necessary spiritual process that in fact fosters wellness.

Progressives believe that education is the key to solving the world's most intransigent problems, like poverty, hunger, and violence. I don't disagree, but I would add that emotional and spiritual education and support is equally foundational. The Slow Grief movement understands that loss is love's conjoined twin, and that loss is, inevitably, a bracingly large component of the human condition. Therefore, until such time as our culture is grief-embracing—and grief openness and support is built into every family, group, and organization—the principles of grief and mourning as well as the skill of empathy must be taught overtly in schools and corporations, much as anti-bullying awareness is taught today.

Just as in the Slow Food movement we take the time to prepare real food and share it with those we care about, in the Slow Grief movement we would take the time to listen to one another without judging and encourage the sharing of internal thoughts and feelings, no matter what they are. After all, if you agree that grief, when fully and openly explored, expressed, and supported, is a transformative experience, you'll probably also agree that this transformation could be harnessed for good. If we helped people in our communities mourn more fully, wouldn't we also be helping them to go on to love more fully? And if we helped them love more fully, wouldn't we quickly be bettering the very fabric of our society?

And in opposition to the international big box store chains, the artisan movement champions local "makers" who sew clothing, cobble shoes, and craft all manner of goods and art. In the Slow Grief movement, I hope we recognize the art of compassionate grief companions like you. The contemporary therapies that are so popular today, billed as "solution-oriented" and "cognitive-behavioral"-based, are all about speed, efficiency, and cognition. They attempt to rid people of their grief symptoms as quickly as possible. Healthcare reform and its focus on time-limited, managed care compounds the problem. The Slow Grief movement supports caregiving that is as slow as the mourner needs it to be as well as heart-based.

A FINAL WORD

GRIEF COMPANIONING IS AN ART, AND LIKE ALL FORMS OF ART, IT TAKES TIME, ATTENTION, PRACTICE, AND PASSION TO GET GOOD AT IT. I myself have been doing it for almost 40 years, yet every mourner I meet has much to teach me.

The philosophy, skills, and sundries we've covered together in this text constitute a particular approach to grief counseling—one that may counter some of the thinking and methods you learned in your formal training. If this is the case for you, I simply ask that you try integrating parts of the companioning model into your work with grieving people and watch what happens.

"Grief is great. Only you and I in this land know that yet. Let us be good to one another."

— C.S. LEWIS

I truly believe that grief companions do some of the most important work there is to do here on this planet. It's hard work, and the pay is incommensurate, but the rewards are nothing short of life-changing for everyone involved. To bear witness as a torn-apart griever slowly and courageously transforms over time into a re-engaged, loved, and loving human being is a privilege surpassed by no other.

Thank you for your commitment to helping your fellow human beings in grief. Without you, many vulnerable people would meander off alone and possibly end up lost for the rest of their lives. But with you and your effective grief companioning skills and ways of being, those in your care who are journeying through grief are never alone, never truly lost, and always in sight of hope.

RECOMMENDED READING

Attig, Thomas. *How We Grieve: Relearning the World, 2ⁿᵈ Edition.* Oxford University Press, 2010.

Bowlby, John. *Loss, Sadness and Depression.* Basic Books, 1982.

Doka, Kenneth. *Disenfranchised Grief: New Directions, Challenges, and Strategies for Practice.* Research Press, 2002.

Doka, Kenneth, and Terry Martin. *Grieving Beyond Gender: Understanding the Ways Men and Women Mourn, 2nd Edition.* Routledge, 2010.

Harris, Darcy; Winokuer, Howard. *Principles and Practice of Grief Counseling, 2ⁿᵈ Edition.* Springer Publishing Company, 2015.

Hooyman, Nancy; Kramer, Betty. *Living Through Loss: Interventions Across the Life Span.* Columbia University Press, 2008.

Klass, Dennis; Silverman, Phyllis; Nickman, Steven. *Continuing Bonds: New Understandings of Grief.* Taylor & Francis, 1996.

Martin, David. *Counseling and Therapy Skills, 3ʳᵈ Edition.* Waveland Press, 2011.

Neimeyer, Robert. *Techniques of Grief Therapy: Creative Practices for Counseling the Bereaved.* Routledge, 2012.

Rando, Therese. *Treatment of Complicated Mourning.* Research Press, 1993.

Rogers, Carl. *On Becoming a Person: A Therapist's View of Psychotherapy.* Mariner Books, 1995.

Rubin, Simon. "The Two-Track Model of Bereavement: Overview, Retrospect, and Prospect." *Death Studies*, December 1999. Volume 23, Issue 8. Pages 681-714.

Savage, John. *Listening and Caring Skills in Ministry: A Guide for Groups and Leaders.* Abingdon Press, 1996.

Stroebe, Margaret, Henk Schut, and Wolfgang Stroebe. "Attachment in Coping with Bereavement: A Theoretical Integration." *Review of General Psychology*, 2005. Volume 9, Issue 1. Pages 48-66..

Walsh, Katherine. *Grief and Loss: Theories and Skills for the Helping Professions, 2nd Edition.* Pearson, 2011.

Wolfelt, Alan. *Companioning the Bereaved: A Soulful Guide for Caregivers.* Companion Press, 2005.

Worden, J. William. *Grief Counseling and Grief Therapy: A Handbook for the Mental Health Practitioner, 4th Edition.* Springer Publishing Company, 2008.

TRAINING AND SPEAKING ENGAGEMENTS

To contact Dr. Wolfelt about speaking engagements or training opportunities with his Center for Loss and Life Transition, email him at DrWolfelt@centerforloss.com.

COMPANIONING THE BEREAVED
A Soulful Guide for Caregivers

This book by one of North America's most respected grief educators presents a model for grief counseling based on his "companioning" principles.

For many mental healthcare providers, grief in contemporary society has been medicalized—perceived as if it were an illness that with proper assessment, diagnosis, and treatment could be cured.

Dr. Wolfelt explains that our modern understanding of grief all too often conveys that at bereavement's "end" the mourner has completed a series of tasks, extinguished pain, and established new relationships. Our psychological models emphasize "recovery" or "resolution" in grief, suggesting a return to "normalcy."

By contrast, this book advocates a model of "companioning" the bereaved, acknowledging that grief forever changes or transforms the mourner's world view. Companioning is not about assessing, analyzing, fixing, or resolving another's grief. Instead, it is about being totally present to the mourner, even being a temporary guardian of his soul. The companioning model is grounded in a "teach me" perspective.

"This outstanding book should be required reading for each and every grief provider. Dr. Wolfelt's philosophy and practice of caregiving helps us understand we don't need to be joined at the head with the mourner, we need to be joined at the heart."
— a grief counselor

ISBN 978-1-879651-41-8 • 191 pages • hardcover • $29.95

ALL DR. WOLFELT'S PUBLICATIONS CAN BE ORDERED BY MAIL FROM:
Companion Press
3735 Broken Bow Road | Fort Collins, CO 80526
(970) 226-6050 | www.centerforloss.com

COMPANIONING THE DYING
A Soulful Guide for Caregivers

By Greg Yoder | Foreword by Alan D. Wolfelt. Ph.D.

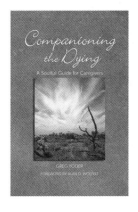

If you work with the dying in your career or as a volunteer, or if you are a family member or friend to someone who is dying, this book presents you with a caregiving philosophy that will help you know how to respond, and what to do with your own powerful emotions. Most of all, this book will help you feel at peace about both your own role as caregiver and the dying person's experience—no matter how it unfolds.

Based on the assumption that all dying experiences belong not to the caregivers but to those who are dying—and that there is no such thing as a "good death" or a "bad death," *Companioning the Dying* helps readers bring a respectful, nonjudgmental presence to the dying while liberating them from self-imposed or popular expectations to say or do the right thing.

Written with candor and wit by hospice counselor Greg Yoder (who has companioned several hundred dying people and their families), *Companioning the Dying* exudes a compassion and a clarity that can only come from intimate work with the dying. The book teaches through real-life stories that will resonate with both experienced clinical professionals as well as laypeople in the throes of caring for a dying loved one.

ISBN 978-1-61722-149-1 • softcover • 148 pages • $19.95

Companion
P R E S S

ALL DR. WOLFELT'S PUBLICATIONS CAN BE ORDERED BY MAIL FROM:
Companion Press
3735 Broken Bow Road | Fort Collins, CO 80526
(970) 226-6050 | www.centerforloss.com

UNDERSTANDING YOUR GRIEF

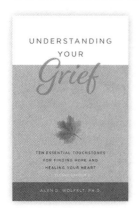

Ten Essential Touchstones for Finding Hope and Healing Your Heart

One of North America's leading grief educators, Dr. Alan Wolfelt has written many books about healing in grief. This book is his most comprehensive, covering the essential lessons that mourners have taught him in his three decades of working with the bereaved.

In compassionate, down-to-earth language, *Understanding Your Grief* describes ten touchstones—or trail markers—that are essential physical, emotional, cognitive, social, and spiritual signs for mourners to look for on their journey through grief.

The Ten Essential Touchstones:

1. Open to the presence of your loss.
2. Dispel misconceptions about grief.
3. Embrace the uniqueness of your grief.
4. Explore your feelings of loss.
5. Recognize you are not crazy.
6. Understand the six needs of mourning.
7. Nurture yourself.
8. Reach out for help.
9. Seek reconciliation, not resolution.
10. Appreciate your transformation.

Think of your grief as a wilderness—a vast, inhospitable forest. You must journey through this wilderness. To find your way out, you must become acquainted with its terrain and learn to follow the sometimes hard-to-find trail that leads to healing. In the wilderness of your grief, the touchstones are your trail markers. They are the signs that let you know you are on the right path. When you learn to identify and rely on the touchstones, you will find your way to hope and healing.

ISBN 978-1-61722-307-5 • 240 pages • softcover • $14.95

Companion
PRESS

ALL DR. WOLFELT'S PUBLICATIONS CAN BE ORDERED BY MAIL FROM:

Companion Press

3735 Broken Bow Road | Fort Collins, CO 80526

(970) 226-6050 | www.centerforloss.com

THE PARADOXES OF MOURNING
Healing Your Grief with Three Forgotten Truths

When it comes to healing after the death of someone loved, our culture has it all wrong. We're told to be strong when what we really need is to be vulnerable. We're told to think positive when what we really need is to befriend the pain. And we're told to seek closure when what we really need is to welcome our natural and necessary grief.

The paradoxes of mourning are three Truths that grieving people used to respect but in the last century seem to have forgotten. In fact, our thinking about loss has gotten so mixed up that the Truths can now seem backward, or paradoxical. Yet the paradoxes are indeed true, and only by giving yourself over to their wisdom can you find your way.

Truth One: You must say hello before you can say goodbye.

Truth Two: You must make friends with the darkness before you can enter the light.

Truth Three: You must go backward before you can go forward.

In the tradition of the Four Agreements and the Seven Habits, this compassionate and inspiring guidebook gives you the three keys that unlock the door to hope and healing.

ISBN 978-1-61722-222-1 • 136 pages • hardcover • $15.95

ALL DR. WOLFELT'S PUBLICATIONS CAN BE ORDERED BY MAIL FROM:
Companion Press
3735 Broken Bow Road | Fort Collins, CO 80526
(970) 226-6050 | www.centerforloss.com

COMPANIONING YOU!
A Soulful Guide to Caring for Yourself
While You Care for the Dying and the Bereaved

Calling all caregivers to the dying and the bereaved!

- Do you generally feel fatigued and lacking in energy?
- Are you getting irritable, impatient, and angry with people around you (home and/or work)?
- Do you feel cynical and detached from the people you companion?
- Do you suffer from more than your share of physical complaints, such as headaches, stomachaches, backaches, and long-lasting colds?
- Do you generally feel depressed or notice sudden fluctuations in your moods?
- Do you feel busy yet sense that you aren't accomplishing much?
- Do you have difficulty concentrating or remembering?
- Do you think you have to be the one to help all those people who are dying or experiencing grief?
- Do you feel less of a sense of satisfaction about your helping efforts than you have in the past?
- Do you feel that you have nothing left to give?

If you've answered yes to any of these questions, or if you know that you need to take better care of yourself but need help getting started, this book is for you. Written by one of the world's most respected grief counselors and death educators, *Companioning You!* affirms the natural challenges of your work while inspiring you to be your own best companion.

ISBN 978-1-61722-166-8 • 128 pages • hardcover • $15.95

Companion
PRESS

ALL DR. WOLFELT'S PUBLICATIONS CAN BE ORDERED BY MAIL FROM:
Companion Press
3735 Broken Bow Road | Fort Collins, CO 80526
(970) 226-6050 | www.centerforloss.com